LET'S TALK

Other books by Jan Paulsen

When the Spirit Descends

Let Your Life So Shine

Where Are We Going?

LET'S TALK

Conversations
With Young Adventists
About Their Church

JAN PAULSEN

Cover design by Gerald Lee Monks
Cover resources from the author
Inside design by Kristin Hansen-Mellish

Copyright © 2013 by Pacific Press® Publishing Association
Printed in the United States of America
All rights reserved

The author assumes full responsibility for the accuracy of all facts and quotations as cited in this book.

Additional copies of this book may be obtained by calling toll-free 1-800-765-6955 or online at http://www.adventistbookcenter.com.

ISBN 13: 978-0-8163-4516-8
ISBN 10: 0-8163-4516-3

13 14 15 16 17 • 5 4 3 2 1

Contents

Thank You

A book of this kind involves the participation of many people. Let me first thank the thousands of youth, young adults, and young professionals from around the world who challenged me through the years of the *Let's Talk* dialogues. It's their ideas, concerns, and hopes that are reflected throughout this book. They are at the heart of our church, and when they speak, the church *must* listen.

A big "thank you" also to Bettina Krause, my assistant. She was a key person, together with Ray Dabrowski, Jennifer Stymiest, John Banks, and Williams Costa Jr., in organizing the *Let's Talk* live broadcasts and Web site. In writing this book I turned to Bettina to research the questions, comments, and challenges the young raised, and these form the backdrop against which some of my comments are made. And then, her editorial skills in bringing it all together.

I also want to acknowledge and commend Pacific Press® Publishing Association, which has been an invaluable partner in bringing this book to the public.

But most of all, I shall always be indebted beyond words to the one and only Lord and Savior, whose love for the young knows no measure.

Jan Paulsen
January 15, 2013

Preface

As General Conference president, I had a conversation with Seventh-day Adventist young people that stretched over seven years and six continents. I spoke with groups of twenty to thirty young men and women at a time—usually college-age students or young professionals—who came together for a one-hour, live, unscripted, unrehearsed conversation broadcast on the church's international television network, the Hope Channel. From Cameroon to the Caribbean, Australia to Germany, Hong Kong to Brazil, these *Let's Talk* broadcasts brought together young people from an incredibly diverse range of cultures, backgrounds, and local church experiences. No topic or question was off the table.

The broadcasts—more than thirty in all—were perhaps the most visible part of the Let's Talk initiative, but behind the scenes there was also the Let's Talk Web site. This site connected Adventist young people around the world with my office in Silver Spring, Maryland, giving them an online space to share their opinions about the church and bringing a constant stream of questions and comments to my desk.

Why? What was the point of these efforts?

From my perspective, I simply wanted to know what Adventist young people were thinking and feeling. The young represent at least half our global family of faith, and they're as much a part of the church as I am. Why shouldn't they have an opportunity to be publicly heard?

I wanted to hear, firsthand, about their experiences—both positive and negative. Was the church failing them in some ways? What could be done better? What were their joys, their frustrations, and their hopes for the future? As a church leader, I felt a need to get a true reading of their "pulse."

From their perspective, I suspect the invitation to have a dialogue with the General Conference president had an element of novelty. Perhaps they were curious to know if their comments would really be unedited and if there were truly no restrictions on topics. I'm not sure many believed this would be the case until the cameras started rolling.

Frankly, when the *Let's Talk* series began, I was pessimistic about where it would take us and, at times, I wondered whether the whole thing would prove to be an embarrassment! What resulted, however, was an ongoing dialogue with our young people that has touched me profoundly in many different ways.

Why do I now feel compelled to bring what I heard during these television and Internet conversations into book form?

In the past couple of years since *Let's Talk* ended, I've had a chance to sit back and reflect on what happened, to consider what these young men and women said to me and what it means—or should mean—to our church.

I wrote this book because I feel a deep sense of responsibility to the thousands of young Adventists I talked or e-mailed with over the years of the Let's Talk initiative. I don't want their ideas, passions, questions, and concerns to disappear into the mist of yesterday's events, soon to be forgotten. By putting some of their comments and questions into writing, my intention is to give some permanence—and perhaps a sense of legitimacy—to the major concerns I heard expressed by our young people.

I also wrote this book because I believe those of us who represent the more "mature" generations in our church sometimes need to be reminded to say less and listen more, to really hear what our kids are telling us.

I came away from every *Let's Talk* broadcast with a strong sense that even though the young and the old in our church may occupy the same pews, we don't necessarily speak the same language. Our experiences, cultural assumptions, and worldviews can be miles apart, and yet we may be completely oblivious to the gulf between us. And then we're surprised when we look around our church and see empty spaces.

My hope is that whether you're young, old, or in between, you'll read this book not as a final word on any particular topic, but as a starting point for a cross-generational conversation in your own family, school, or local congregation. I pray that the ideas expressed by our young people through *Let's Talk* will help you discover the particular burning issues that occupy young people in your local context—for these will vary widely by culture and geography. And finally, I hope this book will help you develop some of the tools you'll need to keep a dynamic and meaningful dialogue going.

As we who are older fade away, a new generation will take our place. What happens next? There will be no church of the future without the creative presence and engagement *today* of those who are young. They're talented, energetic, and spiritually gifted. They want to be involved, for they care about the church.

Please, let's talk!

How to Use This Book

This book is more than just a record of a seven-year conversation with Seventh-day Adventist young people from around the world. And it's certainly meant to be more than just a collection of my reflections on some of the major concerns and themes they raised.

This book is intended as a starting point for a conversation only *you* can continue. You could use this book, for instance, to kick off discussions in your youth group or with students in Adventist schools. You could use it as reading material for your small group meetings, or even as a springboard to start regular Let's Talk events in your local congregation.

But the point is that I hope you'll not just read this book but put it to work.

For this reason, I've included after each chapter a short "Conversation Starters" section with suggestions for how you could continue exploring each topic in a way that makes sense within your local context.

Each Conversation Starter begins with a "Have Your Say" question or activity, designed to draw out the range of perspectives that you'll inevitably find in your discussion group.

This is followed by either one or two suggested discussion questions or activities that will ideally inspire you to consider the issue from new angles.

And finally, each Conversation Starter ends with the question "What now?" and prompts you to consider practical ways that young and old, together, can begin to respond to what you've learned from each other.

Obviously, these Conversation Starters will work best when your discussion group has a good mix of those representing different age groups. But it doesn't really matter: just get the conversation going and see where it—and the Holy Spirit—will take you.

Introduction

In the wake of the Arab Spring uprisings, *Time* magazine named "The Protestor" its 2011 "Person of the Year."[1] In its cover story, the magazine traced the incredible rise of this vast army of young people, bound together through shared grievances and intimately connected through social media. Together, these young people became makers of history—a force that took the world by surprise.

Of course, the idea of a distinct "youth culture" that tests the status quo is nothing new. Significant youth protest movements have marked each decade since the 1960s. And since at least the late 1800s, sociologists of each generation have identified a distinct "young culture"—a period between childhood and mature adulthood marked by rebellion against authority, questioning of traditional values, and a search for identity.

But today's youth culture has an added, unique dimension: a virtually unlimited, globalized communication platform at its fingertips that is profoundly changing the way young people understand and interact with their world. As United Nations Secretary-General Ban Ki-moon said in a recent speech, "As a child, when I first saw a television, I put my hand on the screen because I was fascinated. Now, when my granddaughter sees a TV, she puts her hand on the screen because she expects it to respond to her commands."[2]

Do you know us?

Are we familiar with the current "youth culture" of the Adventist Church around the world? Do we understand the forces of technology and social media that are shaping the thinking and worldviews of the young men and women in our churches? Do we know what's troubling them and what questions they're struggling to resolve? Are we aware of the specific ideas and passions that, for them, define what it means to be Seventh-day Adventist in the twenty-first century?

I suspect the answer, in general, is, "Not so much."

In more than thirty live broadcasts and through the Let's Talk Web site, I heard our young people say, "Do you really hear us? Are you listening?"

Family ties

In every exchange, I was struck by how deeply young people care for their church. It's true that a portion of each broadcast usually dealt with issues that loom large for those working through the challenges of early adulthood—dress, music, dating, and entertainment. Perhaps these topics may strike older people as frivolous or even silly, yet young people must ask these questions along the way toward developing the core values that will guide them through life.

On the whole, however, the issues raised by our young people touched on critical areas for our church as a global family as it moves into a new century.

Really, it's this concept of family that drove the Let's Talk initiative and that I want to bring forward in this book. The Adventist Church is a family, regardless of our vast differences of geography, culture, and language. As in every family, there are young and old who often hold different values and priorities. But we're bonded to each other in love and with a shared purpose, and from this flows a profound sense of support and tolerance for each other.

This idea of family defines the life of a believing community. Yes, we have our doctrines, and we understand the biblical basis for these. We have clear standards of faith, ethics, and morality. But against this static backdrop, church life is shaped by the dynamics of relationships—the give-and-take and often unpredictable interaction between imperfect individuals who've been drawn together into one family.

This is why we need to talk to each other!

Do you really *want* to know us?

This book is structured around the various issues and concerns that kept reappearing in Let's Talk events around the world. At the beginning of each chapter are the voices of the young—I've edited samples of questions and ideas they put before me during broadcasts or through the Let's Talk Web site. Their comments may be surprising to some—perhaps even provocative—and yet, there they are. It's no use trying to gloss over them or make them more "presentable," or we'll invite defeat before we even begin.

After the comments from the young people, I've included some personal reflections on the issues they raise—not in an attempt to put the matter to rest but rather to ask, What can we do about this? Are their points valid? Is what they're saying hostile to the very identity and mission of the church? Is there an inspired word that says No to what they're proposing? Or could it be that if we fail to act on what they're telling us, we'll impoverish our church and obstruct our mission?

Clear messages

I can't claim to have identified some kind of monolithic Adventist youth culture. Such a thing doesn't exist, for the experiences, problems, priorities, and opinions of young people vary dramatically, not just between cultures but *within* each culture as well.

What I did hear through *Let's Talk,* however, was a series of distinct and recurring signals from our young people that, at the very least, should lead us to take note.

These themes included the following:

- The cry of Adventist young people to be accepted as serious participants in the life of the church. "I have ideas, talents, and energies. I want to be heard, understood, and used by my church! If you don't need me, tell me, and I'll be on my way."

- "I don't understand why my church thinks I'm negative and critical simply because I have questions I need to ask. Must I check my brain at the church door in order to be welcome?"

- Standards of dress, diet, relationships, and entertainment. "Is looking drab somehow more Christian? How do I construct a lifestyle I can fully own, and yet that is also fully in line with biblical values?"

- "Why are youth and women—-75 percent of our global family—so underused in our church? The secular world, both in business and government, values the contributions of young professionals and women of all ages, but why don't we? Does God have a problem with this?"

- "This world is where I live today—I can't step out of it. So why doesn't Adventism speak more clearly and courageously to the issues I see in the news media every day? Shouldn't the faith I love have something significant to contribute to matters on the public agenda?"

- "Homosexuality—OK, it's there. I understand the biblical position that shapes our church's teaching about this, but we're talking about human beings, loved by Christ! How can the church uphold its moral and biblical position without appearing strident and intolerant to the point that it doesn't seem to care about people?"

- Cohabitation and sexual relationships outside of marriage. "Are you aware of how 'normal' this is outside the church? Can you please talk to me about why our moral standards and attitudes toward marriage are still valid?"

- "I wish my church could be more tolerant. Having the right formula seems to be more important than how we treat each other. Are being 'right' and being loving mutually exclusive? I look at the way Jesus treated people, and I wonder why doctrinal truth and love for people don't always coexist in my church."

- Through *Let's Talk,* the young revealed a whole spectrum of attitudes about the Bible and Ellen White. There were the enthusiastic idealists who feel we aren't promoting Ellen White's writings as we should; the skeptics who are uncomfortable with her role vis-à-vis the Bible; and the yawning apathy of those who say, "She may have had a role 'back then' but frankly, I don't see that she can contribute anything to my spiritual journey today."

- And then there was the simple refrain I heard from young people no matter what particular issue we were discussing. "Please, let us in the door. Please keep talking with us."

Take a look at the faces of the young men and women you worship with each Sabbath. Do you know what they're really thinking and feeling? You'll never find out unless you ask. This book begins a conversation I hope you'll continue so that it becomes a dynamic, intergenerational exchange of ideas within your family, school, or congregation.

We owe it to each other and to our Lord to keep talking; for when conversation stops, we walk away.

[Endnotes]

1. Kurt Anderson, "The Protester," *Time,* December 14, 2011, accessed December 4, 2012, http://www.time.com/time/specials/packages/article/0,28804,2101745_2102132,00.html.

2. Ban Ki-moon, keynote address to the Global Colloquium of University Presidents at Columbia University, delivered April 2, 2012, accessed November 12, 2012, http://www.un.org/apps/news/infocus/sgspeeches/search_full.asp?statID=1498.

One

Let's Get Acquainted

Sometimes we seem to pass each other as ships in the night—only vaguely aware of the presence of the other. The worlds of the young and the old in our church seem so different. True, the "under thirty" and the "over sixty" occupy much of the same physical space, but within the space of the mind, we could hardly be further apart: our hopes and frustrations; what we rate as important or peripheral; what we see as "alive" or "dead"; our memories of yesterday and visions of tomorrow; and, yes, our choices of entertainment and music.

This reality of separation prompted me to begin the *Let's Talk* television conversation with Adventist young people—a project that developed into a series of thirty-plus live broadcasts taped on six continents. The heart of this initiative was my desire to listen—really listen—to young people and to ask the question: "What does the world, and our church, look like through your eyes?"

The *Let's Talk* series actually began in 2003 with an idea for a single live television broadcast with young people in Simi Valley, California. But from the very first, it became apparent that we couldn't stop with just one interview. The response to that first broadcast made it abundantly clear that young people wanted to talk, that there was a vast, pent-up desire to engage in dialogue about issues important to them and their daily reality.

After more than thirty live broadcasts and a six-year Internet dialogue with young people that brought hundreds of e-mails to my desk each week, I'm left with the conviction that we—the younger and older members of the church—hardly know each other.

Yes, we go to the same church building, we hear the same pastor (although the young don't take from the sermon what the older do), we sing the same hymns (well, some of them), but we hardly know each other. We don't actually talk together. Unfortunately, we're strangers.

The young have a huge need to be heard, understood, and be taken seriously. We need to talk, but those of us from the older generations can't speak to young people as if we're doing them a favor—as if we're magisterially granting them an "audience" with us. We need to admit that not all openness is real, and not all conversations result in genuine communication.

Listen to some of what young people told me through the Let's Talk Web site and through the various *Let's Talk* broadcasts.

- *"I think the best thing church leaders can do for the youth of our church is to get acquainted with them. Too often, church leaders sit on their high horses and judge our youth without having the slightest idea of what they are going through."*

- *"Youth should be given more chances, even though they make mistakes. The problem is that elder folk see some young people's behavior and apply that kind of observation to all the youth. I get the sense they're suspicious of us and our ideas."*

- *"I wish we were encouraged to run projects and programs in the church without people constantly looking over our shoulders and making sure we're doing it 'right.' Parents should be there to cheer the progress and, if criticism is needed, it should be [done] in a loving and building manner, not destructive."*

- *"I think our church elders should schedule a regular time to talk to young people and know about their problems and views on different issues. We don't mind advice and counsel, but I think they should actually listen to us before they give it!"*

- *"Our leaders need to wake up and give the young people more credit. We are more than just globs of emotions, although we're treated that way most of the time. We are thinkers and future leaders."*

- *"I'm not sure if older people realize how condescending they often are to us. They judge us, talk down to us, and squash our ideas. It's time for the 'old folks' to 'let go and let God' when it comes to young people."*

- *"I think the biggest thing young people can bring to the church are new and creative ideas. There are so many more ways the church could be reaching unchurched people, but it seems like the Adventist Church so often just 'talks to itself.' Please, please listen to the ideas young adults have, even if they appear too 'modern' or too 'un-Adventist.' But take those ideas seriously. They just might reach people who otherwise wouldn't hear about the Adventist Church."*

- *"To me, trust is everything. If you trust me and show me that by giving me an opportunity to have responsibility in the church service or in an evangelistic campaign, then I'm not going anywhere! I have at least twenty friends who are all very active in the church because of this. Adults have trusted us with responsibility and we love it!"*

- *"I hate hearing people say, 'Young people are the future of the church.' Really? They have a funny way of showing that."*

- *"I think that instead of always being ready to condemn or judge the way youth think and behave, church leaders should try harder to understand life from the point of view of a youth. I think they've forgotten what it's like."*

- *"Church leaders can make the youth feel valued and involved when their ideas and thoughts are heard and recognized as part of the decision-making process in the church. More often than not, most of the decision making of the church is done by the older ones who give small value to the voices of the youth. In fact, youth are about the last priority in my church."*

- *"We always hear, 'We love our youth, we support our youth' but, really, it never amounts to anything. The way to show that you support us is to actually listen to our ideas, and maybe even let us take leadership of certain things."*

- *"When we [the youth of our church] talk to leaders in the church, they don't really listen—they're hearing us, but they're not open to all arguments and discussion. They always end up doing what they think is important."*

- *"There's a big gap between the young people and church leaders and I don't really see that changing in any meaningful way."*

- *"I'm asking this from the top of my head, and I think that it's an idea that is worth asking. Can we have an 'Exchange Day' where the church leaders and young people switch roles for the day? I think it'll be fun and challenging, but also an experience that will show all of us how each other live."*

- *"The youth of the Adventist Church is a 'sleeping giant.' When we get woken up, it will be powerful."*

This is what they said. How do we handle it?

"Can you hear me?"

There's something powerful in the act of listening. We experienced this truth every time a group of young Adventist men and women and I faced each other at the start of a broadcast. The cameras would roll and we would begin to talk. Sometimes the beginning was slow—the questions were tentative or focused on safe topics. Sometimes the questions betrayed skepticism: "Are older adults really prepared to hear what we have to say?" was the unspoken subtext.

Invariably, though, we experienced a shift as the group warmed up. The young people began to realize that I was there not because I had an agenda or because I had all the answers—sometimes I didn't know the answer and admitted it. But I wanted to hear and understand them—that was all. As we talked, they began to express their pent-up frustration by speaking more freely and with greater passion. And more often than not, our back-and-forth would continue well after the broadcast had ended and the studio lights were turned off.

Through the Let's Talk Web site, the comments from young men and women from around the world tended to be a little "sharper." Perhaps in the relative anonymity of an online forum or an e-mail, these young people felt freer to express the depths of their feelings. In essence, they were asking their church, "Do you really know us? Maybe you think you do, but have you really listened to us? Please, talk to us—before we lose interest in talking to you."

They wanted to talk, but with the goal of being heard and understood. I once had an African student who told me, "I hear you, but I don't hear you." He was saying, "I hear your words, but I really don't follow what you're getting at!"

Maybe the younger and older ones of our church are talking past each other. Maybe we're not even speaking the same language.

Listening for more than words

The young people I met in conversation weren't necessarily looking for unconditional affirmation of their ideas or their opinions—but simply to be heard! To have the chance to express themselves and feel that a leader of their church was seriously listening, regardless of whether I agreed with them or not. To feel that their ideas—and by extension they, themselves—were of tremendous value to their Adventist family. *This* is what fueled the growth of the Let's Talk initiative.

Occasionally, a comment would cross my desk from an older person questioning the value of these conversations, suggesting perhaps that the young people were focused on trivialities or "trying to make huge dilemmas of things that are essentially nonissues. After all, our church is very clear about standards of conduct and what we believe!"

It's true that in most broadcasts some questions were raised—perhaps about dress or hairstyles or entertainment choices—that it could have been easy to dismiss as lightweight or repetitive. But I regarded these questions as teasers to open the conversation. The questions belonged to a broader process in which young people were taking their value system for a test drive. Young people are synthesizing what they've been taught—their "received values"—with their own firsthand experiences as increasingly independent human beings. And in doing so, they're developing a framework of principles that will likely stay with them throughout their lives.

More often, though, the questions reflected serious thought and a genuine desire to understand issues of vital importance for them, personally, and for the church of the future.

First and foremost, the young people wanted the affirmation of someone listening to them respectfully; the assurance that their points of view had legitimacy in the eyes of the church establishment. Before sharing too deeply and before letting themselves become vulnerable, they wanted to know that there were no hidden agendas. This is the underlying message, I believe, in their comments listed earlier in this chapter.

"Are you really listening to us?" they're asking. "Will you try to understand what we're saying? We want to be sure because we've been burnt before."

In summary, I have distilled from the young people's comments a list of things older adults need to understand and do:

- Get better acquainted with your youth—you probably don't really know them.

- Give your youth more chances—second chances, and then some more.

- Thoroughly understand the young people's ideas before judging them.

- If criticism is necessary, offer your comments with love.

- Consider scheduling regular times for discussion with young people in your local church; make it part of the church calendar.

- Admit that young people are thinkers—and they're your future leaders. Treat them as if they are important.

- Avoid sounding condescending, as if you're talking down to them.

- Listen to young people even if they sound too modern and "un-Adventist." They may have ideas for reaching those who are modern and "un-Adventist."

- Trust is really everything. Try trusting them and see what happens.

Are these fair points or not?

When the young people of our church vent their frustration, there's no reason for us to take offense anymore than we would with our own children. It all comes down to a basic question of how we're going to function together as a spiritual family.

They'll have the final say

I also encountered an unmistakably strong, sometimes even brutal, signal from the young in every conversation we had, whether it took place in Manila, Cape Town, or São Paulo. I heard it regardless of whether I was talking with men or women, students or young professionals. I heard it no matter whether we were discussing homosexuality, social justice, racial equality within the church, or women's ordination. It was unmistakable and clear.

It was this: "If our local church is not a place where we're loved, heard, and given meaningful responsibility, then we will walk away."

Young people want their church to be a genuine home, hallmarked by acceptance and love. If it isn't, they'll find it elsewhere. We'll lose them, but not because they've lost faith or they've come undone spiritually or they're "too difficult" or their ideas are too outrageous. They'll leave simply because they feel they don't belong. We'll lose them because we, the older ones, have failed to communicate that this is their church, just as much as it's ours.

I visited many, many churches during my years as General Conference president. Sometimes I'd look out over the congregation, and my eyes would meet a sea of gray hair, and I'd wonder, *Where are the young people?*

Internal bleeding

How many of our young people are we losing? How many have walked out and left without a forwarding address, with perhaps only their immediate family keeping track of what's become of them?

Precise statistics are difficult to find, but according to Roger Dudley, a researcher from Andrews University who has spent more than thirty years studying trends among Adventist young people, some "40 percent to 50 percent of those who are baptized members in their mid-teens will drop out of the church by the time they are halfway through their twenties."[1]

I wouldn't be surprised if 70 to 80 percent of those who were, at one point, students at Adventist schools, are now, ten to fifteen years later, nowhere to be seen. Such numbers are more than alarming—they're catastrophic. They should shake every caring church member awake and make us cry. Our Lord would go looking for one lost sheep; how deeply do we care for the many? Will we make the effort to not just ask the question "Why?" but to actually make changes that need to be made?

We're a mission-focused denomination—we always have been. It's a monumental failure on our part not to be directing more of our resources toward mission by the young, for the young. Let them loose! Just give them resources, support, and trust, and they can do mission among their own peers and friends much more effectively than older "seasoned" workers in mission.

As one young woman said to me, "Trust is what we are asking for." My sense is that they're not actually asking anyone to do anything for them. They just want a climate in which they can thrive, feel accepted, and safe—an environment in which they can cultivate friendships and social lives and which, in turn, becomes the basis for drawing more of their friends, former friends, and colleagues into the embrace of their faith community.

As I think of the ones who've actually walked out the door, I also have to wonder, *How many more young men and women are staying on, one foot in the church and one foot out, unfulfilled in their spiritual walk and unengaged with their local church?* They stay because it gets to be so complicated—socially, with their family, or whatever—to make a formal break.

I doubt there's any single comprehensive plan for reversing the attrition rates of our under thirties. But what I heard from young men and women, over and over again in different ways and in different words, was that we have to look hard at the culture and the "temperature" of each local congregation. Without this first step, we'll have no hope of addressing the bleeding of youth from our churches.

New attitudes

What catalysts could help transform relationships between generations in our churches? Well, here are just a few suggestions.

- Accept the fact that twenty-year-olds will think differently from sixty-year-olds. It's just a fact of life that holds true both inside and outside our church. To deny it or try to override it is insensitive, insulting, and unreal.

- Just as my children and grandchildren are an inseparable part of my life, bonded to me with cords of loyalty and love, so I'm bonded with the young in my church. As with my own family, if they bleed, I bleed. There are no qualifiers—no ifs or buts. If the bond is broken, I suffer.

- The young need space to test the ground of their territory without feeling like someone is constantly looking over their shoulders. This reality means those of us in the older category sometimes need to exercise self-restraint.

- Young people are going to make mistakes; and when they do, we need to love them and embrace them. Let them feel the warmth that comes from us in the midst of the mess they've made. Why? Because they're part of us! We should never walk away in disgust.

- We should never forget that their freedom to make personal choices, even crazy ones, is a freedom God has given them.

- We need the humility to exercise our own gift of remembering. Didn't we also once make the same journey, perhaps many years ago?

This list could be expanded or tailored to your particular congregation, but try these for a start. I believe they'll go a long way toward changing the temperature of intergenerational relationships in your church.

Can we count on any guarantees with respect to outcomes? No. In this, as in all human relationships, there are no guarantees. Will some of our young people continue to go astray? Yes, tragically they will. But by trying on some new attitudes, perhaps we can start keeping more than we lose simply because the atmosphere "at home" makes it a good place for them to be.

Is experience overrated?

And then comes the question I heard over and over again in the *Let's Talk* conversations: "Why can't we be trusted with more responsibility? Why can't we sit on the committees that make decisions? Why can't young adults be much more visible in church leadership, both in my local congregation and in the broader church context? Does the Bible spell out certain age criteria for spiritual leadership?"

What do we say to all this? Usually we say, "With experience comes wisdom and judgment, but the young haven't earned these yet."

But consider this: In 1848, Ellen White experienced a vision that had profound consequences for the development of our church. It's sometimes called the "streams of light" vision. She saw that James White should start publishing a "little paper" that would eventually take the Advent message around the world like streams of light.

What's remarkable to me is not just the vision itself, but Ellen White's actions after she received the vision; her determination to see the Lord's plan put into action in spite of those who said it was impractical, if not impossible. She stood firm against the disapproval of other leaders, such as Joseph Bates, who felt that her husband, James, would be more effective as a preacher than as a writer. She also withstood the doubts of James, who saw the huge financial difficulties involved in printing and distributing such a paper. She insisted: "He must write, write, write, and walk out by faith."[2]

It's easy to forget she was just twenty-one years of age!

When we hand out responsibilities within our local church, experience is often the first criteria we look to, and sometimes with good reason. We want the task done well, and a visible track record is reassuring. But do we tend to overplay the value of experience?

Let's ask first, "How does this person deal with others? Does he or she have the capacity to love and care for the church? Will she or he be responsible? Is he or she prepared to learn? Is his or her commitment strong?"

If you put the right young men or women into a certain place with a defined responsibility, they will gain the experience they need. But put the wrong people in, regardless of age, and they will never do well.

Making trust real

The young in conversation frequently told me, "The older ones in our church don't trust us."

Once we've decided that we're going to entrust an assignment to a young person, our next responsibility is to step back. And then to take another step back. We must do it, risks notwithstanding, because it's right. Only then does the word *trust* name a reality rather than just a buzzword. Micromanagerial supervision has always been a poor model because it belittles and constantly undermines trust. But what if they don't get it right? The simple truth is that young people won't do things by the same methods that we would and they *will* make some mistakes. But making mistakes while being trusted to try something new is a great learning experience.

Sometimes, I suspect our reluctance to allow our young people greater responsibilities within the church stems from motives that have no place within our community of faith—territorialism, the need to control, a desire to wield authority, a feeling that it should be "our way or no way."

Or perhaps our unwillingness comes more from a sense of fear—that our time is over, our contribution will no longer be needed or valued, or our voice will no longer be heard. It's an inescapable fact of life that the moment to step aside will come for a variety of reasons—advancing age, failing health, fading energy, or whatever. Every generation must eventually turn responsibilities over to a younger generation.

There have been moments in my life when I've thought, *How wonderful it might be if I could just hand over my briefcase of responsibilities to those who are half my age.* They have the promises of the prophet (Joel 2:28, 29), a computer full of ideas, and the energies to carry them out. But so often when those of us who are older step aside, our replacement is someone from the slightly-less-old category. It's "safer" that way and causes fewer ripples. It also ensures that there are fewer surprises or innovations. Is this approach less risky and more comfortable? Of course. Could we be closing the door on something extraordinary that the Spirit is seeking to accomplish? I have many moments when I think so.

[**Conversation starters**]

Do you want to explore more deeply some of the issues raised in this chapter? Here are some ideas for getting a dialogue started between younger and older members of your congregation.

1. **Have your say.** What are some of the biggest "trust killers" in the ways older and younger people in the church speak and act toward each other?

2. **Conversation builders.**
   - In a recent survey, young people were asked about the major differences between younger and older generations. They pointed to music, use of technology, political views, moral values, and attitudes toward different races.[3] In your congregation, what are the major differences between the young and the not-so-young?
   - What do younger and older members of your congregation share in common in terms of beliefs, hopes for the church, and vision for mission?

3. **Discussion questions.**
   - How much emphasis should be placed on experience when filling elected positions within your church?
   - Could young people sometimes be partly to blame when they're sidelined from church office? Are they sometimes too passive?
   - What do older people in this congregation need to do or say to make younger members feel loved, heard, and trusted?
   - How can younger people help the older ones feel respected and valued?

What now? What are two or three practical, easily implemented ideas for improving the intergenerational lines of communication within your congregation?

[Endnotes]

1. Roger Dudley, quoted in "180 Symposium Convenes at Andrews," *Andrews University News,* accessed December 3, 2012, http://www.andrews.edu/news/2008/10/symposium.html.

2. Ellen G. White, *Life Sketches of James and Ellen White* (Battle Creek, Mich.: Seventh-day Adventist Publishing Association, 1880), 260.

3. Paul Taylor, Rich Morin, Kim Parker, D'Vera Cohn, and Wendy Wang, *Forty Years After Woodstock, a Gentler Generation Gap* (Washington, D.C.: Pew Research Center, 2009), 4.

Two

"One in Christ—Really?"

[Diversity in the Church]

This is what they said

- *"Pastor Paulsen, I've read what you've written about appreciating diversity in the church. But there are still areas of the world where the church has segregation—I'm talking about the regional conference system in the United States. What is the General Conference doing to eliminate that?"*

- *"Since Jesus Christ our Lord is One, why is the church today still facing challenges of racial division? Pastor Paulsen, what are you doing to get the church united?"*

- *"Recently in our division, two conferences (Trans-Orange and Transvaal Conferences) were to merge. Yet you know as well as I do that blacks walked out of the session because no one in leadership—union, division, or General Conference—wanted to hear their concerns. Leadership was only concerned in making sure the conferences came together. How can we say that we don't discriminate when leadership aren't keen to listen to black brothers as well as white brothers? How can we say that we are a people united in waiting for the coming of Jesus?"*

- *"Pastor Paulsen, I know you're aware of the trouble we've been having here in South Africa. What I would like to know, though, is how the General Conference can judge us and tell us what to do, while there are still black-only conferences in America."*

- *"I live in Florida, and here there is a predominantly Caucasian conference and a predominantly African-American conference that both cover the same geographical area, and which have churches in the same areas. When I think about this my reaction is, 'Really! This is 2009! How can this be?'"*

- *"I find it odd that the wider community seems more in earnest about the issue of racial equality than we do as Adventist Christians. Didn't Christianity write the book on this? So how did we end up so far behind?"*

- *"I've heard that about 70 percent of our church lives in Latin America and in Africa, yet, maybe less than 20 percent of our leadership at the General Conference are natives of those regions. What steps are being taken by the General Conference for our leadership to better reflect the makeup of our church?"*

- *"Non-Adventists here talk about us as the 'American Church.' Please don't misunderstand me when I say that I want to follow Jesus, but that I don't need or want a side-serving of American culture with that."*

- *"Hi, Mr. President. Here in India, you must be aware that people are divided into many castes. These castes are from the social order that existed in the days from Hinduism. What concerns me is that this caste system has taken over the church too. People from different castes attend different churches. Church members marry others only from the same caste. Even promotions in the organization are based on your caste. Now, I would like to know what steps are being taken to rectify this. Is this really how followers of Jesus Christ should be?"*

- *"Here [in New York City] we have black churches, Spanish-speaking churches, Chinese churches—sometimes it feels like we all go to our separate 'clubs' on Sabbath morning."*

- *"I belong to a black church and I'm involved in a lot of ways. But I still find it difficult to feel at home. In my classes at college there are students from many different cultures. It's the same at [the place where I work]. At church, though, race is still an issue and I really don't understand why. And I also don't understand why the Adventist Church doesn't do more to actively discourage racism."*

- *"Hello, Pastor Paulsen. I was one of the students who participated in your Let's Talk broadcast from Andrews University, and you said then that interracial relationships are not biblically wrong. But my dad strongly believes that these relationships are wrong, and he goes on to show where Ellen White writes against them. This is an issue that has torn up our family. It seems that our church has no clear stance on this. But how can a relationship between two people who both believe in the same God, and are committed to the same church, be wrong? Can you help?"*

- *"I go to a Korean Adventist church—my parents are from Korea but I was born here [in the United States]. The problem for me and many of my friends is that we have the expectation of our parents to act in a certain way, and to worship in a certain way. But we don't have the same experience as our parents and we're caught between two different worlds, in a way. For me, at least, it's not easy."*

- *"My [local] church is pretty diverse, and I like that. It's a good mix, overall. But what I don't like is that the different racial groups usually stick together when it comes to 'politics' in the church. I find it frustrating, and I'm really turned off by the way people act sometimes."*

- *"I'm interested in how the church plans to deal with the racial divide that appears to be generational with Seventh-day Adventists. Let's be honest—racist thinking still exists, but it's the younger Adventists who are ultimately going to have to deal with the fallout from this because today's leadership doesn't seem to want to take any action. We have to be authentic about this and deal with it."*

These are questions the young people are asking denominational leaders. What do the paradoxes pointed out indicate, and how do we deal with them?

All is not right

They may be young, but these teens, students, and young professionals are speaking to us about issues they see and experience within their own spiritual family. And they're profoundly troubled.

If I had to name the top concerns I heard from our young people about diversity in the church, I would list the following:

- Why do we continue regional conferences in the United States? Aren't these just relics from the past that divide our church along racial lines for reasons that surely warrant serious challenge today?

- We're told that 70 percent of the global Adventist family is found in Africa and Latin America, and yet, when we look at their presence among the elected leadership at the world headquarters, the fraction is very small. Something doesn't smell right.

- We have ethnic or national churches in many countries, particularly in the Western world. Why can't we worship together rather than dividing along cultural or ethnic lines?

- How exactly does our church plan to deal with the various racial divides that exist in our church? And is church leadership aware that we, the younger generation, have a different take on some of these things than do the older ones in the church?

- Interracial relationships and marriage: Did Ellen White really say these relationships are wrong? What right would she have to say that?

Why are we still struggling with this?

Issues of race and ethnicity are notoriously difficult to address in any context, but it's especially tough to know how to respond to a young person who says to me, "We're followers of Jesus Christ. Why on earth can't we get our house in order on this issue?"

Dr. Martin Luther King Jr. once called the weekly worship service "the most segregated hour in America," and his observation seems to still hold true—not only in America but in many other countries as well. Questions of racial identity and justice in the church can be minefields. This issue comes wrapped in history, culture, habits, likes and dislikes, rights and wrongs. Be sure to factor in emotions and adrenaline, which seem to require no justification to flow.

Questions about race and equality in the Adventist Church surfaced constantly in the *Let's Talk* conversations. Young people have an unfailing ability to find the gap between rhetoric and what they observe in practice, and this discrepancy becomes a question of integrity for them. And they, quite rightly, hold the church and its leadership to the highest standards.

They're asking, When it comes to dealing with the realities of racial and cultural difference, why does my church—both in its message and practice—so often fall short of its ideals? Is equality and unity in Jesus Christ just feel-good talk? Or do we really mean it—even though the ultimate consequences may be disruptive or may not be completely to our liking? Does the notion of equality in Christ inform both our official and unofficial methods of choosing leadership? Is respect for different cultures evident in the way our church operates around the world? Or is one cultural narrative given priority above others?

But it's primarily what happens within their local church community that forms young people's perceptions of how their church relates to racial and ethnic differences. Ultimately, they'll judge for themselves whether "unity in diversity" is indeed an operating principle of Adventism or merely a slogan—a cosmetic fix for differences that run deeper than we're willing to admit.

Young people know what a healthy Christian community should look like—accepting, loving, nonelitist, prepared to embrace cultural differences without a hostile agenda. But what I heard through the Let's Talk initiative was that sometimes our young people see a healthy community modeled within *secular* settings—their school, workplace, social group—more often than within their church family. And the troubling question is Why? Especially when the church should be the ideal place to model God-given values?

No ambiguity

God has said clearly that He doesn't accept historically or socially defined values when it comes to His created beings (Galatians 3:28). These are meaningless as we stand before Him, and nowhere is this more true than among people who share a faith in Jesus Christ. We're bound together in unity as one body in Christ (1 Corinthians 12:13), and by the Cross we're all lifted to a value level that has nothing to do with our education, birth, profession, or nationality. We're one, and we must be protective of each other's status as equally loved children of God. Could Scripture be any clearer on this?

This shared bond—this unity in Christ—is the centerpiece of Adventist identity. We must defer to one another, sacrifice for one another, take joint responsibility for safeguarding what has been entrusted to us. It's a theme that can be traced throughout the ministry and writings of Ellen White. "We should present to the world a united front," she urged believers through the pages of the *Review and Herald* in 1893. "Make it manifest that we are one in Christ Jesus, one with the brethren, bound in covenant relation, under obligation to answer the prayer of Christ to be one in him as he is one with the Father."[1]

And again: "We are to demonstrate to the world that men of every nationality are one in Christ Jesus. Then let us remove every barrier and come into unity in the service of the Master."[2]

Ellen White's clarion call to the General Conference Session in 1891 shines as the clearest of all beacons: "As I knelt in prayer, these words were presented to me as if written with a pen of fire: 'All ye are brethren.' " She was shown the error of those who sought to denigrate the standing of nonwhite church members, and she declared that "the color of the skin does not determine character in the heavenly courts." She added, "Birth, station, nationality, or color cannot elevate or degrade men."[3]

Less than we should be

As we review our church's history of racial, ethnic, and national relations, we must admit that there are chapters we wish weren't there. And we don't need to look just at black-white relations within our church in North America. The blemishes and scars are spread globally.

I recall a visit I made to South Africa in the mid-1980s. Our church was still divided organizationally with two union structures covering essentially the same geographical area—one union covering the white churches, the other, the rest. I traveled for a whole day with the president of the black/colored union, and as we entered one town, nature necessitated that we stop and find a restroom. To my shock (I suppose I should have been prepared), my colleague couldn't enter the same facility I could. I remember my utter disgust as I thought, *For crying out loud, it's just a toilet!* (I have to restrain my choice of words here.) I thought, *How can you dehumanize another person so much that you can't even use the same facility?*

I also think of how our church has behaved, or failed to behave, in the face of tribal or ethnic violence.

In 2005, I visited the Genocide Memorial in Kigali, Rwanda, and laid a wreath in memory of the three-quarters of a million men, women, and children who were slaughtered simply because they belonged to "the other" tribe. We ask, "Why?" and the answers are clinical and cold; they contain no compassion, no Christianity.

How did Adventists in Rwanda respond? Together with many other churches, we failed to be a city of refuge for the innocent. How can people who are "one in Christ" become so destructive toward each other?

I lived in Nigeria with my family in the mid-1960s when the brutal Biafran war was fought. Again, the battlefront was ethnically drawn. Similar scenarios have played out in all their bloody senselessness in Congo, Kenya, Sierra Leone, Ivory Coast, and too many other African nations.

But it isn't just in Africa but in Europe as well. Throughout the 1990s, the multiethnic brutalities in the Balkans left us with the names of cities and places, little known before, now never to be forgotten: Bosnia-Herzegovina, Sarajevo, Srebrenica. And if the church wasn't directly involved, it was tarnished by its silence—the silence of "nonpeacemakers."

After more than fifty years of ministry and international leadership, I'm baffled by the strength of competing ethnic, racial, national, and cultural loyalties within our community of shared faith. Have Christ and the Spirit not been able to temper that? When difficult moments arise and tensions escalate, must Christ always be the loser and loyalty to Him come in second place? What shall we say to Him when we see Him face-to-face?

Let's take a quick look at the questions raised by Adventist young people.

Why do regional conferences exist in the United States?

It's good to remember the history and circumstances that have shaped today's reality of regional conferences. As early as 1928, a group of black ministers proposed that the General Conference "organize colored conferences, whereby the colored people may handle their own money, employ their own workers and so develop administrative ability and all cultural lines of work."[4]

The General Conference wasn't ready to move at that time; but fifteen years later, the momentum was unstoppable. It came against the background of un-Christian and unacceptable racial discrimination experienced by many people at the hands of the church and her institutions. In 1944, a recently formed organization, the National Association for the Advancement of Worldwide Work Among Colored Seventh-day Adventists, petitioned the then General Conference president J. L. McElheney to end racial discrimination in all Adventist institutions. The document appealed to Washington Sanitarium to stop turning away colored people (a term used to refer to any nonwhite people at that time) who sought medical help. (The infamous 1943 experience of Mrs. Byard, who died after being sent away to a "colored" hospital, was a tragic case in point.) It stated that colored girls shouldn't be denied places at Washington Sanitarium School of Nursing, and that Emmanuel Missionary College must end the practice of seating black students at the back during chapel services. The petition also pointed out that there were no black leaders on the staff at Adventist institutions or at the General Conference, and further, our church was lagging significantly behind society. Black people could freely sit and eat where they wished at public and government institutions in Washington, D.C.[5]

From that moment things moved quickly. From 1945 to 1947, seven "regional" (black) conferences were organized. Today, they number nine with a total membership of almost three hundred thousand.

There were clear needs that gave birth to regional conferences in the United States: the need for the church to deal with the stains of racial discriminations, to promote development of leadership, to nurture a sense of fairness in carrying responsibility, and to affirm respect for the spiritual gifts of all members, black or white.

"Haven't regional conferences served their purpose, and shouldn't we now move on as one structurally integrated church?" This was the question that several African American young people, particularly young professionals, put to me in our *Let's Talk* conversations. They point out that a large number of Seventh-day Adventist churches outside the regional conference organizations are well integrated and seem to have harmonious relationships across the racial lines. And, also, as demonstrated in several union conferences in North America, a predominantly white membership constituency will elect African Americans as leaders.

This is a conversation that regional conference leaders and senior African American pastors need to have with their own young adults and professionals, some of whom are reporting to me, "They don't want to talk to us about that."

Perhaps the young professionals need to persist in asking the question because silence creates its own distances, and when conversation ends, people turn away from each other.

Why are so few elected leaders at the General Conference from Africa and Latin America?

It's not happening as quickly as we'd wish, but the number of elected leaders from these regions is increasing at the church's world headquarters. There are legitimate reasons why it's difficult to get a fair and equal representative spread of leaders in place quickly.

- It takes time to grow leaders in their own geographical regions. Being an effective local leader doesn't always translate into effective international leadership.

- Language can be a major hurdle. English is the international language of our church; without some level of fluency in English, good leaders lose their effectiveness in the international milieu.

- Moving and relocating internationally is a major upheaval for families. Some prefer not to make that change.

- Visa and work-permit issues can be a challenge.

My experience has been that General Conference leadership is focused and intentional on trying to improve ethnic representation. Should we be complacent? No—there's more yet to be done.

Why do we seem to encourage national or ethnic churches?

This question refers to national and ethnic churches established by immigrants in their adopted countries. Hundreds of Korean, Mexican, Brazilian, Indian, Ghanaian, Nigerian, and other national churches are thriving predominantly in the United States and Europe.

But for the children of immigrants, these churches can prompt mixed emotions. In the words of one young person who e-mailed me, "The problem for me and my friends is that we have the expectations of our parents to act and worship in a certain way. But they were born elsewhere, and we were born in the United States. We don't have the same experience as our parents, and we're caught between two different worlds."

Ethnic churches preserve the comforting, familiar flavor of a home country, and that's not a bad thing. These churches not only provide a spiritual and social haven for immigrants, but they're often very effective instruments of mission among other immigrants. The connection of a common language is also a big factor.

But ethnic churches are by their very nature transition churches, established for good reasons and meeting the needs of specific members of the Adventist community. These needs relate primarily to first-generation immigrants. The needs of later generations are different. For the children of immigrants, their home country is where they were born. Their friends, schooling, and social life all belong to the "new world."

Interracial marriage: Is that bad?

Perhaps I'm defensive on this question: My youngest son is married to a daughter of Africa. We've been blessed with a wonderful daughter-in-law who is the mother to our three much-loved young grandsons.

Yes, I'm aware of the counsel provided by Ellen White cautioning against interracial marriage.[6] I think it's important, though, to consider the note provided by the White Estate at the General Conference.[7] It says, in effect, that to gain a right understanding of Mrs. White's meaning, you need to read her comments on interracial relationships against the background of her many other statements about race. And when you do, it becomes clear that her counsel on interracial marriage is not an issue of racial inequality. She's speaking instead to the question of the advisability or inadvisability of these relationships in light of the circumstances and conditions of her time, where such relationships could produce controversy, confusion, and bitterness.

Any marriage involves bridge-building between two individuals and two families. The greater the distance between the two at the beginning, whether through differences of ethnicity, language, culture, or religious values, the more challenging the task they have ahead to make it work. Sometimes the stresses are too great.

But no matter what their ethnic heritage, two human beings who've come to know and love each other, who stand equal before God and before each other, have the opportunity to make marriage an amazing union.

A generational challenge?

Is the issue of racial inequality really a generational issue within our church?

Yes, it is to the extent that our young people are citizens of an increasingly postracial global society. Obviously, the denomination is not yet postracial—not even close—but nonetheless, that's the direction in which society is moving.

Young Adventist men and women see that in our increasingly globalized, "flattened" world, someone's ethnic origins may be interesting, but that race is functionally irrelevant in everything that really matters.

And so they ask, quite legitimately, "Why does the culture inside my church sometimes look different? Why is the body of Christ being left behind by secular society on this issue?" They have little understanding or tolerance for the ways in which the church continues to fall short.

My grandsons are growing up speaking three languages—French, English, and Norwegian—and for them, this is quite natural and normal. So far in their short lives, they've lived in three countries and experienced many more different cultures. How should I explain to them the structural inequalities—relics of an era long departed—that exist within their church?

We are sons and daughters of a heavenly Father who says to us, "You have no right to assess the value of other human beings. I've shown you unmistakably that *every* person is infinitely valuable to Me."

We are one people, equal before God, bonded in Christ, and destined to live eternally as brothers and sisters.

[Conversation starters]

Do you want to explore more deeply some of the issues raised in this chapter? Here are some ideas for starting a dialogue between younger and older members of your congregation.

1. **Have your say.** How well does the Seventh-day Adventist Church demonstrate Christ's "radical equality"?

2. **Conversation builders.**
   - According to Tankiso Letseli, the first black president of the church's Helderberg College in postapartheid South Africa, Adventists should be ahead of secular society when it comes to race relations. He says we must be "agents of change, instead of merely responding to change."[8] Are Adventists followers or leaders when it comes to breaking down racial divisions?

   - In a recent roundtable on race relations, Christian writer and pastor Tim Keller suggested that converting individuals to Christianity doesn't eliminate racism. Rather, he argued, structures and systems play a big part in allowing racism to flourish.[9] Do you think he's right? What could this suggest for how we tackle racial divisions within our church?

3. **Discussion questions.**
   - Do significant tension points of culture, race, or ethnicity exist within your congregation?

   - To what extent are differences and tensions inevitable—even healthy—within the body of Christ?

   - If someone from your community visited your church on Sabbath morning, how would the worship service look through his or her eyes? Do you think your congregation would seem an inclusive, welcoming place for minorities?

   - Would it be helpful for the Adventist Church to be more deliberate in acknowledging its past and present failures to "practice what we preach" when it comes to race relations?

What now? What are some *personal* changes in attitudes or beliefs as well as *structural* changes in your local congregation that would help your faith community better demonstrate equality in Christ?

[Endnotes]

1. Ellen G. White, "Brotherly Love Needed," *Review and Herald* 70, no. 42 (October 24, 1893): 662.

2. Ellen G. White, *Testimonies for the Church,* vol. 9 (Mountain View, Calif.: Pacific Press® Publishing Association, 1948), 196.

3. Ellen G. White, *The Southern Work* (Washington, D.C.: Review and Herald® Publishing Association, 1966), 12, 13.

4. Quoted in Jacob Justiss, *Angels in Ebony* (Toledo, Ohio: Jet Printing Services, 1975), 46.

5. "Shall the Four Freedoms Function Among Seventh-day Adventists" (a petition drafted by the Committee for the Advancement of World-Wide Work Among Colored Seventh-day Adventists, April 1944), cited in Delbert Baker, *Telling the Story, an Anthology on the Development of the Black SDA Work: A Collection of Historical Documents, Articles, and Visuals on Selected Topics Relevant to the Black SDA Work* (Loma Linda, Calif.: Loma Linda Printing Services, 1996), 2/10–16.

6. Ellen G. White, *Selected Messages* (Washington, D.C.: Review and Herald®, 1958), 2:343.

7. Ibid., 2:343.

8. Quoted in Chantal and Gerald Klingbeil, "More Than Skin Deep," *Adventist World,* November 2011, 19.

9. Katherine T. Phan, "John Piper, Tim Keller Discuss Why Churches Still Struggle With Racism," *Christian Post,* March 30, 2012, accessed November 2, 2012, http://global.christianpost.com/news/john-piper-tim-keller-discuss-why-churches-still-struggle-with-racism-72364/#qT63FLEhIZ6VPS6e.99.

Three

"For Now, This World Is My Home"

This is what they said

- *"When I was growing up, I definitely got the sense that we had to be completely focused on the Second Coming when Jesus would come and destroy the world and make everything new. Now I feel that we sometimes use that as an excuse to do nothing to improve things. Environment? Hunger? Economic justice? Doesn't matter; everything's going up in smoke eventually."*

- *"Our churches seem like 'self-contained bubbles' where people inside pretend that issues from the real world don't exist—drug use, homosexuality, materialism, sex, and relationship issues."*

- *"Adventists—actually Christians, generally—can be their own worst enemies. We're so busy telling everyone what a mess the world is in, and what everyone is doing wrong, but we're not prepared to actually go out on a limb to do something about it. I think we lose credibility for that—when the 'sinners' seem more concerned about fixing what's wrong with the world than we are."*

- *"Why is it that the pope receives global media coverage for advocating peace when you, as our church president, stay silent? What efforts, if any, are being made by the world Adventist Church to promote global peace and harmony?"*

- *"The Adventist Church hasn't always been at the front of social or racial reform. But why not? Do you think we as Adventists should engage ourselves politically to change society?"*

- *"What are we doing about world poverty, and specifically about the situation in Darfur?"*

- *"I've read our church statement on the environment, and I have to say my reaction was basically, 'That's it? Is that all we have to say?' (Not to mention that the statement is more than a decade old, and I've never heard of anything else 'official' about this issue.) I've been told over and over again since Primary Sabbath School that every Sabbath we celebrate God's creation of the world, so I would have thought that we'd have something a bit more substantial to say about looking after what God made."*

- *"When I look at how [another denomination] is really known for getting out and talking about the environment and why it matters for Christians, it makes me wonder if our church would ever do something like that. I wish we would."*

- *"I'd really like to see us become more vocal in the media if we can about hard issues and what we stand for. We need to be courageous. Obviously, that's a risk, and we may be misquoted or something, but we should be out there and be recognized as people making a stand."*

- *"I can understand to a certain extent why the church doesn't come out with a statement on something like the Iraq War. But isn't there a danger that the church will become culturally irrelevant if it continues to ignore difficult issues?"*

- *"I'm sorry if this is offensive, but why are we trying so hard to pretend we're living in the 1950s rather than the twenty-first century? While we're trying to turn the clock back, we're losing the chance to actually do something meaningful about so many other things, like poverty."*

- *"When I read the Bible, I get the impression that if Jesus Christ was on earth today, He'd also be very interested in other problems we see around us."*

- *"I sit through the sermon every week, and really I'm struggling to know how what the pastor is saying makes any difference to what I experience every day. I really feel like there's a big, gaping hole between what we talk about on Sabbath and what 99 percent of the population is really interested in."*

- *"I'm seeing that the church is a lot more interested in being on the safe side of any given topic, than having anything real to say. Really, that embarrasses me. The middle of the road may be safer, but it isn't where I see Jesus walking."*

- *"Our message about tobacco use, healthy eating, and so on used to be ahead of the times, but these things have pretty much become mainstream now. We used to be noncombatants and conscientious objectors, but no one in the church really talks about that anymore."*

- *"We hear a lot about evangelism and soul winning as if that's the extent of our mission—not that I'm against evangelism. I just find it very disturbing that we have so much to say about people's souls and so little to say about the world people live in."*

- *"I'm from Haiti and there are so many poor people in my country and around the world. Why aren't we as a church doing more for poor people?"*

- *"Adventists used to be a 'movement,' and now I feel that we're just another institution that's mainly about doing things the same way we've always done them. We've really lost sight of mission, as in dealing with the down-trodden and poor people of this country."*

This is the church speaking to the church. What does it mean and how do we deal with it?

"It's just a stage they're going through"

Should we dismiss appeals such as these as idealistic? Naïve? As demonstrating a misplaced focus, which could be better directed toward the evangelistic mission of our church? Do we simply assume, "They'll grow out of it"?

Of all the ways we could react, condescension is probably the most dangerous. If faced with a dismissive attitude on the part of their elders, our young people may surprise us by growing out of their Adventist faith, rather than abandoning their impulse toward social engagement.

Throughout the Let's Talk initiative, the sheer intensity and strength of the call by Adventist young people for our church to become involved in issues that engage society was surprising. Their appeals, whether on the broadcasts or through the Web site, were strong and consistent: "Why isn't the Seventh-day Adventist Church—my church—more 'real,' more 'visible,' more 'active,' more 'relevant' in the public sphere?" The reasoning of the young is simple and irresistible: "We cannot step out of society. This is where we live. So, we have to care—somehow."

The invisible church?

It's clear that our church can't tackle every single social ill it may encounter, and nor should it try. The task is too large and too complex. And trying to be relevant, simply for relevance's sake, is a very poor rationale indeed for any church engagement—whether at the world church level or within a local congregation.

But, on the other hand, I believe that embracing irrelevance, whether through fear of engaging with complex issues or through simple inertia, is an inexcusable abdication of our God-given mission. We've been called to be God's "salt" in society (Matthew 5:13–16); we're to spread out and season our communities with values shaped by eternity. The alternative is to simply stick together and form a salty, indigestible lump—functionally alien to the everyday challenges and sufferings of people. Unfortunately, that's exactly how some of our young people perceive their church—isolated from reality and uninterested in engaging with issues such as environmentalism, poverty, peacemaking, fighting racism and injustice, or HIV/AIDS—issues that impact the lives of multiple millions around the world.

The young people's frustration seemed to be compounded by their passionate belief that *Adventism shouldn't be like that*—that it actually does have something unique and important to contribute both to the public discourse and practical initiatives. They feel that so many elements of the public agenda should properly be on ours as well, for these things aren't at odds with our values or mission.

Putting Adventism to work

The young people gave a strong impression that, on the whole, the relevance they seek is not a watering down of their faith or an attempt to make it indistinguishable from the world around them. Instead, they want their faith and their church to have practical significance—here, today, where they live, work, and do mission. They want Adventism to be a part of the suffering world, not to stand aloof from it, as if unwilling to share in the suffering or in fear of being tainted. They aren't looking to diminish our message; they just want to amplify it and put it to work.

And so, their search for relevance is not necessarily symptomatic of an anemic faith. On the contrary, it signals a depth and strength of commitment that compels them to ask, "Why wouldn't Adventism have something meaningful to say about issues that drive the public agenda?"

As I've reflected on my conversations and e-mail correspondence, I've come to believe that what these young people were really expressing to me was their struggle with what they perceive as credibility gaps or disconnects between the values they've been taught and their observations of how our church interfaces with the public sphere.

In an online comment, one of the Let's Talk participants referred disparagingly to an official church statement about peacemaking, calling it "all talk, no action." In 2002, my colleagues and I on the General Conference Executive Committee voted the statement, called "A Seventh-day Adventist Call for Peace." It's one of some fifty-plus statements our church has issued over the years on social issues as diverse as religious freedom, assault weapons, and contraception. In it, we expressed our conviction that Adventists are called to be peacemakers in society. We called on church leaders and members to recognize the social and political forces that destabilize our communities—poverty, war, terrorism, and more—and to take a more active role in fostering peace and stability, and enhancing the quality of life.[1]

I was conscious then, as I am now, that official church statements are not an adequate replacement for involvement, and that the label of peacemaker must be earned, not simply claimed. Does this make our Call for Peace any less grounded in Adventist convictions and biblical values? Of course not. Is there value in is-suing official statements highlighting how God's people should relate to broader society? Yes, I believe there is. I believe there's value and nobility in simply being a moral voice for good causes—such as the plight of the poor or the suffering of refugees—even if the size of the task is too big for us as a church to fix.

The reality is that our church has a limited pool of resources, and so we must prioritize our efforts. As an administrator, I understand this. Yet it can be diffi-cult to communicate this to young people without it sounding like a convenient escape hatch. As I talked with our young people, it was clear they longed for a greater congruity between what their church says is important and the way it actually sets priorities and allocates resources. They want feet-on-the-ground, get-hands-dirty action. In the words of Christian social activist Tom Davis, this is a generation that craves a "faith that bleeds."[2] And if they don't see that their church has real, practical significance in addressing the world in which they live, their embarrassment and pain is such that they may ultimately walk away.

For me, the Let's Talk initiative confirmed beyond a doubt that Adventist young people have an infallible radar system for detecting empty talk. They have a well-honed moral sensibility and a deeply grounded sense of fairness. If the gap grows too large between what they hear in the pews and what they observe in the way their church relates to social ills, they can—and do—become disillusioned and cynical.

Is there a disconnect between church reality and the real world?

Over the course of the Let's Talk conversations, young people described their church as "isolated," "in a bubble," "looking inward," "too focused on ourselves," "blind to what's happening," "not interested in anything but ourselves," and "separate from the rest of the world."

Are we really? Are these fair comments?

Maybe we recognize something that arises out of our theology—a mind-set that perhaps at times we've cultivated. Could it be that sometimes our firm belief in the soon second coming of our Lord and our great desire to get His people ready blinds us to other aspects of our mission?

The question of one participant in a *Let's Talk* Africa broadcast has stuck with me. "Have you ever visited in the home of a poor person? I mean a really poor person?" he asked me. And I had to say, "No, I haven't." Yes, I grew up in an occupied country during the Second World War when food was often in short supply. I remember days when I experienced the pangs of hunger. But I don't have a genuine understanding of the day-to-day experience of the grinding, heartbreaking poverty that leaves a parent with a gaunt face, empty eyes, holding a crying child in her arms whose hunger she can't relieve.

The young people of our church are asking us, Are we willing to "visit" in the world long enough to really understand the issues and distresses that define reality for much of the world's population? When we preach, does what we say recognize what's happening outside our church doors, or do we sometimes nurture the attitude of a reclusive community?

Is there a disconnect between Christ's example and our priorities?

In his commencement address to Harvard University's 2001 graduating class, singer and social activist Bono said, somewhat acerbically, "Isn't 'Love thy neighbor' in the global village so inconvenient?"[3]

He's right. There are potentially uncomfortable implications in Christ's command to "love our neighbor" in the context of our tightly interconnected, rapidly shrinking world. Our neighbor has become not just someone who lives in our town or nation, but also the person dying of HIV/AIDS in Mozambique, who doesn't have access to medicines that are readily available in the West; the child working in a sweatshop in Asia to produce clothing for the markets of the United States and Europe; a woman eking out a subsistence for her family in the slums of a big city. As globalization remakes our world's economic, social, and political structures, will the church bring biblical values and principles to bear in this rapidly changing landscape? Or will we, like the priest and the Levite, pass by on the other side of the road?

Bono has taken on a self-appointed role of "conscience" to the world's political and religious leaders through his relentless campaign to funnel more resources from the West to victims of HIV/AIDS in Africa. "Christ's example is being demeaned by the church if they ignore the new leprosy, which is AIDS," he said in one interview. "The church is the sleeping giant here. If it wakes up to what's really going on in the rest of the world, it has a real role to play. If it doesn't, it will be irrelevant."[4]

His indictment captures the spirit of what Adventist young people are saying.

They keep asking, "Is our church awake to what's happening in the world? Do we see? Do we realize that there's genocide, preventable starvation and disease, massive economic and social inequalities, unthinkable suffering through war or repression of basic human rights?"

Young people are not necessarily asking their church to fix everything; they're simply asking if their church is committed to taking Christ's example seriously. Are we looking at what's happening around the world through Christ's eyes? And if not, why not? To what extent are the defining questions of our Lord in Matthew 25 catalysts that lead us to act? "I was hungry; I was naked; I was in prison; I suffered from loneliness; I was ill; I was an addict. Did you care enough to come and talk to Me and touch Me?"

Many young people see a certain irony, also, in the middle-class respectability that marks so many of us who claim to follow the One who regularly shook up the social and religious establishment. There was a genuine puzzlement in the voice of a young man who asked during the *Let's Talk* Washington, D.C., program, "We claim to be followers of Jesus Christ, but I don't see that the church is really that interested in the 'untouchables' in our society. You know, today's tax collectors and prostitutes. I just don't see it."

Is there a disconnect between our past and present?

On more than one occasion, I've been confronted with a comment that goes something like this: "The early pioneers of our church weren't afraid to speak out publicly or even to wade into the political fray for a cause they believed in. So what's happened to us? Why do we today always keep our 'heads down' when it comes to public action?" There's a sense that, compared with the passionate and prophetic voices of our spiritual forebears, we've become insipid and much too cautious in our engagement with public issues.

Repairing the disconnections

Why are these perceived disconnections so distressing for many of our young people? They're yearning for an integrated faith—a force that's not contained just in their heads or their hearts, but that colors every part of their day-to-day experience. Talking the talk is not enough. For them, it's imperative that convictions and deeds go hand-in-hand.

In the jargon of sociologists, Adventist young people between the ages of eighteen and thirty years of age fall under the label of "Millennials"—sometimes also called "Mosaics," or "Gen Ys." And two of the characteristics researchers consistently find present most strongly within this generation are a deep concern for social justice, combined with a longing for meaning and significance in their lives.

They want to make a difference! Their commitment to principles is not weak, insipid, or imprecise. No, I find it to be quite strong and clear, but it's coupled with an equally strong desire to see those principles at work and making a practical difference in the world around them.

Some may respond, "Such an attitude largely reflects the aspirations of each new generation!" Yes, perhaps. Yet there's an additional factor to consider: this generation of young people has also shown that, when confronted by an institution or idea that doesn't work—that fails to have a visible, practical impact in their lives—they'll take the nearest exit. They're gone. They'll reject traditional institutions that seem irrelevant. It's a trend revealed by numerous broad-based studies of Generation Y, which show a dramatic drop in the number of young people who claim a specific religious affiliation.[5]

How do we address this call for relevance? How can we do a better job at not just talking about but demonstrating Adventism's concern for the whole person, our conviction that no aspect of human life lies beyond Christ's touch; no facet of human activity falls outside the scope of His care?

This is our heritage as Seventh-day Adventists, and our task isn't static. We have a continuing responsibility to engage with emerging concerns in society and to bring our distinct values and prophetic voice to bear on those things that impact the communities in which we live today. Why? Because "Christ identifies His interest with that of suffering humanity. . . .

"Will the church arouse? Will its members come into sympathy with Christ, so they will have His tenderness for all the sheep and lambs of His fold?"[6]

[Conversation starters]

Do you want to explore more deeply some of the issues raised in this chapter? Here are some ideas for starting a dialogue between younger and older members of your congregation.

1. **Have your say.** Is being active in social issues or being engaged with questions on the public agenda a distraction from our mission?

2. **Conversation builders.**
   - According to Christian blogger Caleb Trimble, " 'culturally relevant' is the most ambiguous phrase known to mankind."[7] When people urge the church to be more culturally relevant, what changes do you think they're looking for?

   - In a recent *Wall Street Journal* article, the author says some Christian churches try to be "cool" by constantly referencing pop culture or by staying on the cutting edge of technology. Yet, he writes, "As a twenty-something, I can say with confidence that when it comes to church, we don't want cool as much as we want real."[8] What's the difference between a church that's trying to be "cool" and a church that's trying to be "real"?

3. **Discussion questions.**
   - Could our convictions about end-time events sometimes contribute to a sense of isolation from society—a bunker mentality?

   - Adventist pioneers spoke against slavery and advocated for noncombatancy and religious liberty. Today, are there social issues that particularly mesh with Adventist values—issues that would allow us to make a unique contribution?

   - Would your community notice if your church suddenly wasn't there? Or would your disappearance have no noticeable impact on the day-to-day life in your neighborhood?

   - Are there any dangers for the church in taking up issues on the public agenda?

What now? Is there a project your local church or youth group could take on that would help make Adventist values *real* to your community?

[Endnotes]

1. "A Seventh-day Adventist Call for Peace," voted by the General Conference Executive Committee on April 18, 2002, Silver Spring, Maryland.

2. Tom Davis, *Red Letters: Living a Faith That Bleeds* (Colorado Springs, Colo.: David C. Cook Communications, 2007).

3. "Commencement 2001: 'My Name is Bono, and I Am a Rock Star,'" *Harvard Magazine,* July-August 2001, accessed December 4, 2012, http://harvardmagazine.com/2001/07/bono-speeches-commencement-2001.

4. Quoted in Wesley Campbell and Stephen Court, *Be a Hero: The Battle for Mercy and Social Justice* (Shippensburg, Penn.: Destiny Image Publishers, 2004), 32.

5. Paul Taylor and Scott Keeter, eds., *Millennials: A Portrait of Generation Next* (Washington, D.C.: Pew Research Center, 2010), 85.

6. Ellen G. White, *Welfare Ministry* (Washington, D.C.: Review and Herald®, 1952), 23, 24.

7. Caleb Trimble, "Culturally Relevant: The Most Ambiguous Phrase Known to Mankind," *CalebTrimble* (blog), October 4, 2010, accessed December 4, 2012, http://calebtrimble.blogspot.com/2010/10/culturally-relevant-most-ambiguous.html.

8. Brett McCraken, "The Perils of 'Wannabe Cool' Christianity," *Wall Street Journal,* August 13, 2010, accessed November 3, 2012, http://online.wsj.com/article/SB10001424052748704111704575353311122648100.html.

[Four]

"Let Us Serve the Lord!"

[Women in Ministry]

This is what they said

- *"It's difficult for me to take the church's agenda seriously. I mean, my church tells me that simply because I'm female I can't be ordained to pastoral ministry. So regardless [of] how clearly I hear God's call to ministry, my service to Him— at least within my church—has to fit within a certain 'box.' "*

- *"What I don't understand is why no one in leadership seems to want to address [the request by women to serve as ordained ministers]. I realize that we're a global church, and I understand that many places just aren't ready to move forward with this; that the cultural context means having women serving as pastors would actually do more harm than good. But what about places where excluding women from ministry marks our church as out of step and culturally irrelevant?"*

- *"It is incredible to see those who argue 'for' or 'against' women's ordination fire their biblical arguments back and forth. And it seems like such an inconsistent use of Scripture. People just stretch and contort what the Bible says to suit their own perspective. For instance, how many of those opponents of women's ordination who quote Paul's dicta that women must remain quiet and cover their heads and so on, actually follow this to the letter? They're [already] interpreting this, to some extent, within the cultural and historical context of Paul's time. Yet, they somehow interpret his words to mean that women in the twenty-first century Adventist Church can lead a Sabbath School lesson but can't be a fully recognized pastor."*

- *"I find it incredibly ironic that a church that owes so much to the spiritual leadership of a woman should be so resistant to the idea of women taking leadership roles within our church today. Can't they see their own hypocrisy in this issue?"*

- *"Regardless of how the question of women's ordination is decided, what bothers me the most is that our church is set up so that, structurally, the fact that women can't be ordained automatically filters them out from a significant proportion of leadership roles. The ordination track is so central in our church to grooming people for leadership, exposing them to leadership experience and service on leadership committees, and so forth. Basically, then, it's a self-perpetuating boys' club!"*

- *"Frankly, I'm not interested in arguing this point anymore. The chances of convincing someone—who genuinely believes the Bible accords women a second-class status when it comes to ministry—is minimal, if not nil. Their cultural presuppositions blind them to any other understanding. So really, what's the point? Society has moved on, and I will too."*

This is our church talking to us. What should we say in reply?

"No comment" is not an option

What has stayed with me from my conversations with Adventist young people is how deeply many of them care about the question of women in ministry. Their comments were, by turns, incredulous, passionate, and brutally honest in expressing their points of view. Their feelings and convictions were grounded in what, for them, were strong biblical and moral arguments. The validity of their viewpoints can be argued, but the genuineness of their convictions cannot. The young will accept—in this, as in so many other issues they raise—that they could be wrong, but they want to hear the arguments, and they want to see the basis on which their stand should be rejected. And that demand is fair and reasonable, isn't it?

Obviously, there's no single, united view among Adventist young people about the question of women in church leadership or ministry. Many individuals, particularly from non-Western cultures but also from the West, either don't see this as a pressing issue or dismiss it as something that's politically driven by a women's rights movement. Others firmly believe that faithfulness to God and His Word demand that ordination to the gospel ministry be reserved for men.

But without exception, in every *Let's Talk* television conversation, I met this issue in one form or another. Young people want to know whether, and how, their church is planning to move forward on this; what it means for the future of the Advent movement; how women in ministry—or their absence—affects our ability to speak effectively, transparently, and genuinely to society. They ask, "How can we best pursue our mission in *our culture and our time?*" Their point is that faithfulness to God is expressed and can be real only within the culture and time in which each of us lives. We shouldn't prostrate ourselves before arguments that belong to a different culture and time unless there's a clear "Thus saith the Lord" that establishes a law that's timeless and cultureless. This line of reasoning is difficult to fault.

The "when and where" of faithfulness

Clearly, the pressing issue in the minds of so many of our younger members is, Why can't the church affirm both the promise and the fact that the Spirit has been poured out, indiscriminately and in equal measure, on both our "sons and daughters" (Joel 2:28)? How can this reality be translated into faithfulness and effectiveness in mission in the *culture and time where we live?* It can only be "where we live," for that's the only place where we function for God, worship Him, and engage in mission.

We must admit that on many different issues, our church has sometimes made comprehensive statements about situations and cultures elsewhere; and we've done this with an instructive spirit, which says "thou shalt" or "thou shalt not." We've argued, "This is what works where I am; it must also work for you."

The flaws in this reasoning are clear. When it comes to mission and spiritual life, only an unambiguous "Thus saith the Lord," broadly accepted as timeless and applicable across cultures, will be accepted. Anything less will be resisted as alien, unworkable, and possibly even offensive. And for each of us, obedience to God is personal, and it must be obedience where we live.

Help! Please explain it to me

Take another look at the comments that begin this chapter. The tone and spirit of the questions are challenging but respectful, even as we sense frustration and, at times, maybe a touch of anger. Many of our young truly feel that church leaders are stuck in a viewpoint and with a perspective that's unsupported by a "final" word of inspiration.

Sometimes proponents of women's ordination are stereotyped as strident feminists who belong to a movement full of "angry lesbians who want to be men."[1] Over the years, I've been questioned by many young people, in many different settings, and I can't remember meeting one individual who fits this description.

These young people uniformly expressed their concerns intelligently and with a genuine desire to understand. Frustrated, disappointed, and a bit bewildered, they ask me, "Why does the church I belong to hold this position? I'm challenged by colleagues and friends, and I don't know what to say! I'm embarrassed. With the Bible in my hand, I can explain the Sabbath, the second coming of Christ, the health message, but I cannot deal with our stand on women in ministry and leadership. Help me!"

And, interestingly, I find that young men are equally as dismayed as women by this wholesale discrimination within their church against more than 50 percent of its membership.

During the last of these live *Let's Talk* conversations, held in Washington, D.C., in early 2010, a young man asked, "When is the church going to address the issue of women and ordination? And do you believe that women should not be ordained?"

In my answer, I acknowledged that the church had studied the issue at various times and settings during the past thirty years and had found no clear, unequivocal endorsement of one position or the other, either in the Scriptures or in the writings of Ellen White.

I explained that for Adventists, ordination to the gospel ministry is understood as a global endorsement, effective wherever the minister is called to work. And I talked about the high value we place on unity and our efforts to find worldwide consensus on this issue. I explained that regional solutions will inevitably bring other consequences in their wake.

But I also said I knew of no biblical reason why women can't be recognized in ministry just as fully as men are. Women offer strong, creative participation in the life of the local congregation, I told him, and a church that denies their participation in congregational life and leadership is robbing itself of gifts God has entrusted to the community of faith.

Later, I found out that my questioner was an attorney in his late twenties who was employed in a high-level position in a government agency. He'd attended an Ivy League law school, although his interest in spiritual matters had also led him to earn a theology degree along his route of study.

Did my response satisfy him? Probably not. At that point in his life's journey, my answer probably didn't mean that much to him. Why? Because every day of his life he is surrounded by young professionals, such as himself, whose competence and ability are assessed by criteria that have nothing to do with gender. In fact, I had the impression that he was interested in my response, but somewhat dispassionate about the issue itself because he had moved beyond waiting for the church to change—or even wanting it to change. He'd come to the realization that the church would do what it would do, regardless of how he felt about the matter. Was I looking at apathy in this very smart and gifted young man?

Apathy!

Apathy is what church leaders should fear far more than the most impassioned, emotionally charged debate on women's ordination. For the many Adventist young people who live and work in a society that has moved well beyond the question of women's equality, they sadly say, "We don't need the church's blessing on this matter." They've resigned. Hope has become too distant and unreal. And, if they see no sign of the church moving on this issue, they, themselves, will simply move on. To many of them, the church is in danger of becoming, at least on this issue, morally bankrupt. They look to society and see a level of functional and professional equality that seems so natural and obvious that it doesn't need to be defended. And then they look to the church, which holds the Bible in its hands, and ask, "Why? What has gone wrong?"

It's not that they believe cultural norms should decide rights and wrongs. No, they're clear about that. The young people I talked with knew that Scripture and the inspired message of the Lord's servant must help us decide what's right. They have no quarrel with this being the gold standard that overrides any issue of culture. But, they request, show us the authoritative Word of inspiration on this question.

And in the absence of an acceptable response along comes apathy.

We can't afford for apathy to set in among our youth and young professionals. In some parts of the world, it may already be too late, and we face a monumental task to reverse the indifference. Our Bible scholars and leaders can sit loftily and proclaim our particular interpretation of a given passage, which someone else will quickly interpret differently, while, at the same time, we see valued, gifted, energetic, and potentially creative members of our faith community just giving us a yawn of indifference and saying, "Who cares?"

Seeking biblical direction

And so here is the unavoidable challenge to church leadership: Is there a message from God to help us find our way in this matter?

In seeking an answer to that question, we should briefly recognize the history of the various study groups established by our church to consider the question of women's ordination. Further, we should identify the biblical passages and reference points often used by those on both sides of the argument. And then, last, we need to look at how we're to understand ordination itself.

Brief though this discussion must necessarily be, we can't leave this issue without at least suggesting a potential way forward. We can't just keep on talking. Talking still hasn't taken us anywhere in this matter. It hangs there unresolved in the not-yet-ready rubric. If the Bible doesn't stop us, when and how can the role of women in ministry and leadership be moved beyond *not yet* and brought into the life of the church *today*?

It seems we can find good counsel in the rule outlined by James White in 1860 and apparently endorsed by Ellen White: "All means which, according to sound judgment, will advance the cause of truth, and are not forbidden by plain scripture declarations, should be employed."[2]

Historical background

Since the very beginning of the Advent movement, our pioneers recognized the role of women as important partners in the mission of the church. In the 1870s, women were licensed as ministers and their task was evangelism—the preaching and teaching of the truth of the Bible. Even three decades before the well-documented ministry of Lulu Wightman, who carried a ministerial license and was a most successful minister, the delegates at the 1871 General Conference Session voted that "means should be taken to encourage and properly instruct men and women for the work of teaching the word of God."[3] They were to "instruct our devoted young men and women, all over the land, in the principles of present truth, and the best methods of teaching them to the people."[4]

Clearly they were not talking here about just school teachers, health workers, or social services—they're clearly talking about the ministry of teaching and preaching the biblical message. "Devoted young men and women" were held together in this assignment. And ten years later, at the 1881 session, the delegates considered a proposal that "females possessing the necessary qualifications to fill that position, may, with perfect propriety, be set apart by ordination to the work of the Christian ministry."[5] Again, the assignment they're talking about is clearly the spiritual ministry of preaching and teaching the Word. After some discussion, the matter was referred to the three General Conference officers for further attention. There it apparently died.

Ellen White's landmark statement a few years later in 1895 should be noted:

> Women who are willing to consecrate some of their time to the service of the Lord should be appointed to visit the sick, look after the young, and minister to the necessities of the poor. They should be set apart to this work by prayer and laying on of hands. . . . If they are devoted women, . . . they will be a power for good in the church. This is another means of strengthening and building up the church. We need to branch out more in our methods of labor. Not a hand should be bound, not a soul discouraged, not a voice should be hushed; let every individual labor, privately or publicly, to help forward this grand work.[6]

The broadness and inclusiveness of this statement must not be overlooked. The appeal to "branch out more in our methods" and that "not a voice should be hushed . . . privately or publicly" surely signals an engagement in ministry that also includes women.

Treading water?

The role of women in ministry and leadership in our church has been on the agenda, on and off, formally and informally, since the end of the nineteenth century. However, during the past four decades, it has come up more frequently. But being on the agenda has *not* meant that the issue has been moving deliberately toward some resolution, and such lack of progress is troubling. We just talk and talk, as we've done since the 1973 Mohaven Conference submitted its report to Annual Council, and we say, "This must be studied some more." Commissions and study groups have met—three such just in the 1980s—with the recommendation coming to the 1990 General Conference Session that women not be ordained to the gospel ministry.

Some progress was made on functions (but not *status*) of women in ministry by the Annual Council action of 1985, which authorized women, qualified through regular ministerial training, to be employed and to perform essentially the functions of an ordained minister.

The sticky question has always been, Is there a clear biblical basis, or counsel from Ellen White, that would support, or at least guide, the church in bringing women into ministry and leadership within the church on an equal footing with men? The world church has never been able to reach a consensus that has enabled it to say, "Yes, we think there's a way."

This reality was again illustrated at the 2011 Annual Council when the executive committee voted not to provide for an expanded functional role in leadership for women.

What should be patently clear is that questions about the role and functions of women in ministry aren't going away, and can't simply be met with silence.

So, what are the big issues or obstacles that keep emerging? Is there no way to resolve them?

[1. A biblical preclusion?]

Some would hold that we should not move forward for biblical reasons. They argue that both the Creation story as well as the language describing the male-female relationship after the Fall (Genesis 1–3) give man a constitutional authority over woman, to rule over her and keep her in subjection to him.

Headship?

Careful scholarship, though, tells us this isn't a valid position, as demonstrated clearly in Gerhard Hasel's paper "Man and Woman in Genesis 1–3," prepared for the meeting of the Commission in 1976.[7] He first establishes that "both man and woman share their creation in 'the image of God' which lifts them above all other creatures and places them together in a special relationship to God,"[8] and he examines the use of specific words that describe the man-woman interrelationships. He then says, "Gen 1-2 would seem to indicate the equality of man and woman, that these chapters militate against the notions of superiority or inferiority on the part of either man or woman."[9] He concludes, also, that the order in which man and woman were created doesn't imply notions of superiority or inferiority.

Did the Fall change any of this? How are we to understand God's statement to Adam and Eve that "he shall rule over you" (Genesis 3:16, NKJV)? However one interprets this, the context is clearly marriage (although it may be a strain to understand it even there!). Again, Hasel concludes: "This divine declaration does not apply to all spheres of woman's life and activity [and] cannot be used to support male domination and supremacy in all spheres of life."[10]

Even when applied to the marriage relationship, it's good to remember that love, harmony, and the notion of equality is what binds a marriage together. The headship notion is defined by the relationship of God the Father to His Son, Jesus Christ. Whatever "headship" means, it never destroys the notion of equality; at best it could be thought of as the first among equals.

Very appropriately, Dr. Hasel closes his paper by saying that the church is responsible "to establish equality and unity in the human family where there is now inequality and disunity. . . . Does the urgency of the task and the shortness of time not require the total utilization of all of our manpower and womanpower resources in the completion of the gospel commission?"[11]

Clearly, Gerhard Hasel, a highly respected biblical scholar in our church, finds nothing in Genesis chapters 1–3 that should prevent women from being ordained to ministry or be barred from holding leadership positions in the church.

"Neither male nor female"

Then, how are we to understand Paul's statements touching on this question?

The passages that come to mind are 1 Corinthians 11:2ff., 1 Corinthians 14:34, 35, and 1 Timothy 2:12; and then, of course, Galatians 3:28, which some would consider of pivotal importance in addressing the respective status of men and women in the Christian community. Is there a clear signal from these passages that speaks to us *today* and can be considered normative for how we should resolve the issue of the role of women in the life and mission of the church?

However you understand Galatians 3:28—that in Christ there is neither "male nor female," for all believers "are one in Christ"—this doesn't do away with functional differences between male and female. But it does reject any notion of male dominance over female or any sense of female inferiority. In Christ, manhood and womanhood are lifted up to an equal plane of value, regardless of obvious physiological differences that impact roles and functions, and differences impacted by time, culture, and local conventions. These differences must be understood without in any way qualifying or destroying equality.

I don't think we're entitled to use Paul's statement in Galatians 3 to say that it, alone, clears the way for the ordination of women. Paul is dealing with the much larger issue of how we view and relate to each other within the church. However, the role of women in the church may be part of that larger issue, and, hence, there may be a compelling argument for bringing this passage into the discussion.

Frankly, if we're looking for a single passage, any passage, in the New Testament that clearly takes us to the ordination of women to ministry, I think we'll be searching in vain.

Contradictions?

What, then, do we do with the apparent tensions between passages in 1 Corinthians 11 and 1 Corinthians 14? In chapter 11, Paul recognizes, or at least doesn't deny, that in certain circumstances it may be appropriate for women to pray and prophesy in a public setting, while in chapter 14, he specifically denies women the right to speak in public.

Some have attempted to resolve the apparent conflict between these two passages by suggesting that Paul directs the command for women to be quiet in public to those who were disrupting the public worship service by "chatting from the balcony." That would be a strained interpretation of Paul's use of the Greek word *lalein,* and it's an interpretation that doesn't stand up under scrutiny.

No, Paul is clearly recognizing that there's a setting and circumstance when it's appropriate for a woman to speak in a worship service. How, then, does this fit with his very clear statement in 1 Corinthians 14:34, 35 that women should be quiet in the public service?

I would suggest that Paul has two different gatherings in mind. When he allows women to speak and bring a message from the Lord ("prophesying"), he has in mind a closed meeting of the believers. We know there were house meetings in the early church (Romans 16:5; 1 Corinthians 16:19) where believers came together in a closed, protected setting, probably to celebrate the Lord's Supper. But these were proper church services. A woman believer with a message from the Lord was free to speak.

But other meetings conducted by the church were open to the larger public. This was part of the mission of taking the gospel to the Gentiles. In this setting,

Paul specifically says that the women should be quiet (1 Corinthians 14). For a woman to stand up to preach and teach in an open meeting would not be well received by the general public at that time.

The gospel itself was enough of a stumbling block, and the church, then as always, had to act with good judgment. It had to take care, in both teaching and conduct, not to give its enemies any unnecessary fodder for scandal. In admonishing women to remain silent, Paul is sensitive to the potential accusation that Christianity is breaking down the conventions of society—destroying marriage, home, and society.

I suggest it's from this perspective that we should also understand 1 Timothy 2:11, 12. The pro and con schools with reference to women in ministry usually focus on both Galatians 3:28 and 1 Timothy 2:11–13. Some try to reconcile whatever tension there is between the two passages by saying we shouldn't bar women from preaching and teaching in the church, so long as they don't do so "authoritatively"! Whatever that means, it seems contrived. If your teaching or preaching doesn't have implicit authority, hadn't you better sit down?

What has all of this to do with ordination to ministry today? It's quite a stretch to make that connection! Today, we're far beyond the point of women being silent in public. And the very most one could make out of these Pauline passages relates to not preaching or teaching in a public gathering—although culture, then and now, must guide in the application of this counsel.

What is absolutely clear, however, is that redemption in Christ has brought men and women to an equal standing in the eyes of God. Baptism is the "magical" moment when this is realized.

[2. Cultural obstacles]

Culture doesn't stand still—it's a constantly shifting force that is shaping and reshaping the dynamics of our environment. Culture varies with both time and location. The culture of the first-century church is no longer the culture in which we live *today*. And we can't help but live and function for Christ where we are *now*. Different cultural perspectives may be interesting to study, but they relate to other worlds. Whether secular or religious, past conventions of society—such as views on slavery and women as well as on circumcision—are no longer values by which we define what should or shouldn't happen today.

The gospel, as it was communicated among both Gentiles and Jews by the early believers, was vulnerable. It was new and radically different from other established religions. As history abundantly illustrates, both the Christian faith and its early adherents quickly became victims. Christianity contains society-and-culture-changing values, but these changes take time to accomplish.

Maybe Paul hadn't worked out the details in his own mind and maybe he hadn't got it all together, but he was concerned that the early believers shouldn't give the enemies of the church unnecessary ammunition. In that culture and time, a woman's role in public was subdued. Paul's counsel to the believers was that this norm should be respected. The principle was good—then and now: you're free, but don't flout your freedom to your own destruction or to discredit the community to which you belong!

The search for cultural consensus

Culture is the one obstacle we're up against today in trying to define acceptable roles for women in the life and mission of the church. The voices of our youth in particular demand that we face this and deal with it.

Perhaps we should have realized in 1990—the first time in recent years that this matter was brought to a General Conference session—that we couldn't resolve this question in a uniform way within a worldwide church family that embraces so many different cultures.

Clearly, it's too simplistic to say, "This isn't a biblical issue but a cultural one." A clean division between the two is difficult to sustain. The Bible and culture work together. Was not Paul's counsel to the early believers: "Find some harmony with the culture in which you live; do your best to respect what's there, and recognize that even change toward that which is better may be a slow process"?

We should have known that there was no way our church around the world, in one fell swoop, could make a massive cross-cultural decision regarding the role of women in ministry. Our global community, while one in faith, is vastly diverse in many ways. Our experiences, our education, and our journeys have been different. Conventions and laws differ between nations. How can we expect Europe to say what's acceptable in Latin America, or Africa what should apply in North America? In the absence of an unequivocal Word of the Lord, which crosses all times and cultures, we must both respect and live with local conventions.

When it comes to the role of women in the ministry in our church, there's no such Word of the Lord. And so the church everywhere must ask, How can we most effectively and faithfully do mission where we are?

[3. Understanding ordination]

Arising from the Mohaven Conference in 1973, a recommendation went to the Annual Council that the "election of women to local church offices which require ordination" should be recognized and supported, in areas of the world church that are receptive to such action. The recommendation refers to Ellen

White's statement of 1895 that such women "should be set apart . . . by prayer and the laying on of hands." This provision for women being elected and ordained as local church elders quickly found its way into the policy books of the church.

Subsequent commissions set out to explore an extended role for women in the pastoral ministry of the church, and were no doubt aware of Ellen White's later counsel that "it is the accompaniment of the Holy Spirit of God that prepares workers, both men and women, to become pastors to the flock of God."[12]

And so in 1989, the Annual Council took the action that women who've gone through the appropriate ministerial training may be employed in pastoral ministry, but without ordination. Ordination would clear the way for full functional participation in ministry, including organizing new churches, ordaining ministers, and serving as conference presidents.

It's all about mission

It should be clear at this point that, as a church, we've moved well past asking whether or not it's appropriate for women to preach and teach in public (the issues raised by Paul in 1 Corinthians and 1 Timothy). By our actions, we've affirmed the vital role of women in the life and ministry of our church. At the same time, we've recognized that in some places public preaching and teaching by women simply wouldn't help the mission of the church.

The determining factors in these situations are local conventions and customs—*not* a biblical injunction.

Hence, the pivotal question regarding women in ministry within the Adventist Church is no longer one of *function,* but of *status.* Should women who engage in ministry be ordained or not?

And this takes us to the critical question of mission, which is the assignment the Lord has given to us. Within the cultural kaleidoscope of our world, how can we best and most effectively do mission? Unity of faith and spiritual identity don't require uniformity of action (see Acts 15). We're not required to do mission the same way everywhere—we can't. But somehow, we must be sensitive to what society will accept without scandalizing the church.

As a missionary movement, we must constantly remember that "the fields are ripe for harvest." We all need to give of our best and let the gifts of the Spirit, which have been given to every believer, play out in the mission of the church.

If the problem is no longer centered around functions—to which Paul may have objected in his time—but *status,* we must ask, "What does ordination bring to candidates that isn't already present in the call God has given them, the spiritual gifts they display, and the authorization of the church to go and work? Are we putting a meaning into ordination that belongs neither to Scripture nor our own history?"

Still talking

So, where does limiting the discussion to status take us, and where do we go from here?

The General Conference Executive Committee has voted to undertake a comprehensive review of our understanding of ordination. The findings of this process are meant to help the church move beyond our current impasse. Fair-minded people—even those who feel that the meaning of *ordination* is clear and who wonder what this additional study can resolve—will prayerfully await the outcome of that study.

Perhaps the greatest value of this process lies in the fact that it keeps the conversation going and it has educational value. When conversation ends, people walk away from each other. That must not happen to us.

As we wait, it's good for us to remember that our youth and young adults particularly are aware of the world outside our church. This is where they live, work, and play. They see a world that's anxious to demonstrate the equality of women. This is the reality of their culture. And many of them are telling us they feel spiritually and morally compromised by staying in a church that can't affirm women in ministry and leadership on an equal footing with men. They know we've never said, as a church, that there's a biblical injunction that prevents us from moving forward. We've discussed it, we've studied it, we've noted differences of opinions, but we've never said that the Bible gives us a clear No.

So, their natural question is, "Why can't the church ordain women wherever culture permits?"

Indeed, why not?

[Conversation starters]

Do you want to explore more deeply some of the issues raised in this chapter? Here are some ideas for starting a dialogue between younger and older members of your congregation.

1. **Have your say.** How would your congregation react to having a woman as senior pastor?

2. **Conversation builders.**
   - Beyond what you find in Scripture, do you think other influences have helped shape your feelings about women's ordination?

   - An online petition urges Seventh-day Adventists to support "Christ" versus "culture" by opposing the ordination of women to ministry.[13] Is this a helpful or unhelpful way to frame this issue?

   - What happens during an ordination service? Does the new pastor receive special spiritual powers, such as the power to pronounce forgiveness of sin? Does ordination involve a transfer of apostolic power to the new pastor? Or is the church simply acknowledging that God has called this person to pastoral ministry, and saying, "Now, go to work!" Does our understanding of this make a difference to our discussion of women's ordination?

3. **Discussion questions.**
   - Do you think the unity of the worldwide Adventist Church depends on sharing one approach to the issue of women's ordination?

   - Would ordaining women to gospel ministry in your area boost your church's ability to do mission? Or would it harm your mission agenda?

   - When talking about women's ordination, do we tend to caricature or belittle those who hold a different opinion to ours, making it even harder to find common ground? Do individuals on both sides of the discussion sometimes need an attitude check?

   - How could you encourage a young person who says, "I'm tired of waiting for my church to get itself together on this issue"?

What now? Could your local congregation be more inclusive when it comes to women in ministry leadership? What steps could you take to more clearly affirm the spiritual gifts of all church members?

LET'S TALK

[Endnotes]

1. See Jared Wright, "Doug Batchelor's 28 Fundamental Arguments Against Women Ministers," *Spectrum Magazine* (blog), March 19, 2010, accessed December 4, 2012, http://spectrummagazine.org/node/2253/.

2. James White, "Making Us a Name," *Review and Herald,* April 26, 1860, 180.

3. Action of the 1871 General Conference Session, cited in Bert Haloviak, "Longing for the Pastorate: Ministry in 19th Century Adventism," General Conference Archives, 1988, 3, 4.

4. Ibid.

5. Twentieth Annual Session General Conference of Seventh-day Adventists, December 1, 1881, General Conference Archives: 197—GCS, 63–88.

6. Ellen G. White, "The Duty of the Minister and the People," *Review and Herald,* July 9, 1895.

7. Gerhard Hasel, "Man and Woman in Genesis 1-3," in *Symposium on the Role of Women in the Church,* ed. Gordon M. Hyde et al. (Washington, D.C.: Biblical Research Institute Committee, 1984), 9–21.

8. Ibid., 19.

9. Ibid., 23.

10. Ibid., 27.

11. Ibid., 29.

12. Ellen G. White, "Canvassers as Gospel Evangelists," *Review and Herald,* January 15, 1901.

13. Online petition by Advent Voices, Shaking Time Ministry, accessed December 3, 2012, http://adventistvoice.com/2012/06/14/christ-or-culture-crisis-adventist-ordination/.

Five

"No Thinking Allowed?"

[Faith and the Questions We Ask]

This is what they said

- *"Everyone has their own relationship with God, and their own faith, and when something comes up that seems to challenge these things, people get passionate fast. So I understand why people feel threatened by science that doesn't support the Bible's story of Creation. Personally, I'm past that. I don't feel that [a belief in evolution] makes me unqualified to be a Christian or an Adventist."*

- *"My comment is that the church doesn't do a good job of explaining this [apparent conflict between faith and scientific orthodoxy] to young people. . . . I think we're smarter than many older people think. We just need to be given better explanations."*

- *"It really bothers me when people I respect a lot—people in my church—have an instantly bad reaction to any discussion about evolution or the age of the earth. Can't we at least talk about it without people thinking we've gone off the tracks for even wanting to raise the issues?"*

- *"The way I see it is that the Bible is open to interpretation, including the story in Genesis of Creation. Christians can't even agree on what the Bible is really saying, and that just adds to the confusion about the evolution and creation debate. I don't see that the average, nonscientist person can make sense of it all."*

- *"I'm a biology major at [an Adventist tertiary institution]. We have to study the theory of evolution because it's 'scientific orthodoxy,' but overall we're taught biology from a creationist perspective. I'm trying to come up with something to put the two together in a way that makes sense, but I'm not sure that it can be done."*

- *"Why does everyone get so fanatical about the creation/evolution argument? So long as we're sure that God was somehow involved in the process, I don't think it matters how He did it or whether it took a week or millions of years."*

- *"This is what makes me uncomfortable. We start with a 'given' that the Creation took six literal days and that there was an actual worldwide flood, and then we try to make the scientific evidence fit around this assumption, or we simply ignore anything that can't be made to fit. I don't think this is a very credible way to approach scientific inquiry."*

- *"What annoys me is when people use 'faith' as a cop-out for really dealing with some of the difficult questions that science raises. So they say, 'You just have to have faith!' and it gives them an excuse to simply ignore anything that contradicts what they believe."*

- *"Here are my only choices—believe in the Bible's story of Creation or believe the scientific evidence, which seems to point to an evolutionary process. Basically, I'm being asked to choose between my faith and what I'm taught is true at school—and there's not a lot of room there for 'gray' areas. I'm not sure if I'm ready to jump one way or the other. My question is, Is it OK to just say 'I don't know'?"*

- *"I believe that God created the world in six days, but I also find it embarrassing to see how Christians are shown in the media as having closed minds and being anti-science. We have an image problem! We need to be able to show people that you can be smart and be a Christian too."*

- *"If you said you believe in a literal six-day Creation on my [non-Adventist] campus, people would just laugh at you."*

This is the church speaking to the church. How should we respond?

The private world of the mind

I remember one of my students at Newbold College in the 1970s—a brilliant young man whose supple intellect marked him as one destined for academic success. He graduated from the theology program, married, and entered the ministry—set on a course, it seemed, for a life of service to God and to the church. I had such a good feeling about him: his faith and spiritual vision as well as the direction he'd chosen for his life professionally.

But some years later, in the early 1980s, events in the broader Adventist Church set in motion a theological "shaking" in some quarters, with a focus on 1844 and Christ's mediatorial ministry. Many of our best and brightest became unsettled, and I received a call from this young man's conference president. "Can you come and talk with him?" the president asked. So I traveled to meet with my former student, and as we talked, he shared with me some of the questions and doubts that were relentlessly undermining both his ministry and his faith.

"But are these questions all new?" I asked him. "Did you not struggle with some of these things during your days as a theology student?"

Yes, he answered. He *had* wrestled with questions, even as he'd sat and excelled in my classes at Newbold.

"But why didn't you tell me?" I asked. "Why didn't you open up and talk with me? Maybe we could have worked through these things together! Maybe we could have resolved what you have clearly not resolved on your own?"

And then I had to quietly ask *myself* some probing questions: Did those who were my students not feel safe in opening up and talking with me about their inner struggles? Would their futures as workers in the church have been in jeopardy if they confessed to struggles with doubts? Would they have been socially vulnerable in our church by admitting such things? Is it too risky for anyone in our church to admit to probing other ways of thinking?

Ultimately, it became clear that it was too late to save this young man for the Adventist ministry—he had come adrift, an outcome that causes me pain even today. Could I have done more for him? Perhaps—and that is my problem.

Troublesome gray areas

As humans, we must sometimes contend with faith tinged with doubt, with convictions accompanied by niggling questions, and with certainty that's mixed with dregs of uncertainty. Should that surprise anyone? We are admitting to no more than being human beings. God made us free—with the capacity to think. So, if you're alive, you think! (Although admittedly, some of us sometimes seem barely alive!)

And more than this, each of us is constantly exposed to change—both in the external realities of the world around us and in the internal world of our own minds. We grow, we gain experience, we encounter new people and new ideas. We meet arguments whose freshness and newness we find striking. We mature, our perspectives change, our assumptions shift. But through it all, our core beliefs—those which define our faith and essential worldview—must be robust enough to survive these inevitable moments when the human mind exercises its God-given capacities. Our faith identity must be able to withstand difficult questions, filled with uncertainties, and endure no matter where our exploration of established positions takes us.

Is this something to be feared?

If you mean, "Are there risks in it?" Then yes, there are. Living a risk-free life isn't possible. Our minds process ideas and generate creative thoughts, some of which will take us on journeys where the destination can't be presumed. That's just the way it is! The autonomy of the mind is risky business. Those who've never wrestled with doubt or with perplexing questions are probably either in denial or have permanently parked their intellect in neutral.

Real consequences

There can be no doubt that how we choose to engage with challenging questions can have a potentially devastating impact on our spirituality and our faith. The critical question in this context is, What discipline or controls are in place to guide the autonomous exercises of the mind?

You may have friends, parents, or mentors who will help guide the process, but, ultimately, the controls are in your own hands. Difficult as that may be, the alternative—letting others control the workings of your mind—is fraught with even greater uncertainties and is wholly unsafe.

For bright, educated Seventh-day Adventist young people—many of whom may have been nurtured within a believing family, a church school, and a close-knit faith community—their first real, sustained encounter with ideas and philosophies hostile to Adventist beliefs can be intellectually brutal. They're confronted with data and conclusions—antithetical to their faith and for which they may be totally unprepared—presented by credible, knowledgeable individuals who seem to represent intellectual and scientific orthodoxy. It can be a bewildering, disorienting experience. This surfaced clearly in the questions and comments which the young raised.

What are they to do with these new, disturbing ideas? Will they be seen as disloyal if they express these ideas to others in their church? Is the mere fact that they have questions or doubts evidence that their faith is somehow inadequate or unstable? As Adventist Christians, can they maintain both intellectual integrity *and* spiritual integrity? Or are they expected, as one young man suggested to me, to "park their brains at the church door"?

Honoring God with our minds

Handling this matter is not only a challenge for our young people but a serious issue for the church and its leaders. We were never meant to issue intellectual straitjackets at the church door or at the entrances to our academic communities.

As a church, we've been encouraged to develop thinkers. The consistent counsel of Ellen White is that "the truths of the divine word can be best appreciated by an intellectual Christian. Christ can be best glorified by those who serve Him intelligently. The great object of education is to enable us to use the powers which God has given us in such a manner as will best represent the religion of the Bible and promote the glory of God."[1]

This isn't a uniquely Adventist issue. A recent survey of Christian young people in the United States addressed the question of science and faith. Of the more than one thousand eighteen- to twenty-nine-year-old Christians who were interviewed, 42 percent felt that "churches are out of step with the scientific world we live in"; 34 percent characterized Christianity as "anti-science"; 34 percent said they'd been "turned off by the creation-versus-evolution debate"; and 29 percent felt that "Christianity makes complex things too simple."[2]

Throughout the Let's Talk initiative, a few young men and women suggested that being an Adventist required one to wear intellectual blinders and that genuine academic inquiry was incompatible with strong faith. Many more, however, were clear on what they believed, and yet they said, "It's tough being a Christian in a world which often derides our faith, especially when it comes to questions of the origins of the earth and life. Frankly, I sometimes feel out of my depth."

Please, give us the tools we need

The *Let's Talk* conversations clearly revealed that Adventist young people generally have a strong sense of loyalty to their faith, and they want to articulate it clearly and intelligently when it's assailed by antagonistic forces. "Church-bashing" is not their agenda. They're jealously protective of their church.

But they're undeniably challenged. They're not always clear as to how they should respond to voices that tell them they're out of step with reality. They're in their formative years—either at universities or establishing themselves in their professions—and they're bombarded from all sides with values and viewpoints, many of which they find difficult to reconcile with their faith.

Whatever we do, let's never imply to our young people that asking questions and seeking answers is somehow unholy or unworthy of a believer. What many young Adventists are looking for is not just an understanding of incredibly complex issues, but for a clear assurance from their church that what they're going through is normal and healthy. Is giving them this assurance too much to ask?

I expect that in this matter, as in so many other issues that concern our young people, they don't necessarily expect us to have all the answers. For them, it's more important that they can have a genuine conversation, that they feel they've been understood and respected, and that their loyalty to the Lord is not being questioned.

Nurturing faith *and* intellect

What can we as a church do to provide a more supportive environment for our young people as they struggle with some of these questions? Are there specific steps we could take to increase the chance that they'll come through with their faith not only intact, but stronger? Let's look at four starting points.

1. Reject anti-intellectualism. According to the late author and atheist Christopher Hitchens, "Faith is the surrender of the mind; it's the surrender of reason."[3]

Similarly, Richard Dawkins, the well-known apostle of evolutionary biology, has called faith the "great cop-out, the great excuse to evade the need to think and evaluate evidence."[4] Are they right? Does a "surrender of the mind" correctly describe your faith experience? Is anti-intellectualism an inevitable by-product of belief in God, His work as Creator, and His role in both our day-to-day life and the affairs of nations—in short, any display of His presence that can't be scientifically tested? Is there a fundamental hostility between faith and the workings of the mind?

Absolutely not! A faith that parks the intellect somewhere has deprived itself of the instrument by which God communicates with us. God doesn't bypass the mind. We can't make decisions that are congruent with God's purpose without a mind that's fully engaged and receptive to His messages.

Therefore, to say to our youth "just be quiet and believe" is not only an insult; it's fundamentally unhelpful and unsafe to their spiritual development. They'll ask, they'll question, and they'll challenge, for that is their God-given right. The beauty and strength of truth must be its personal discovery by each believer, a result of his or her own search.

A hiding-our-heads-in-the-sand approach may feel more comfortable when we're faced with challenges to our faith, but it's a stance that Ellen White clearly rejected. "Ignorance will not increase the humility or spirituality of any professed follower of Christ," she wrote. "The truths of the divine word can be best appreciated by an intellectual Christian. Christ can be best glorified by those who serve him intelligently."[5]

Indeed, Adventism has strong roots in the tradition of rigorous, independent inquiry. "Those who have entered upon the work of teaching, or who have been called to any position of responsibility, should not be satisfied to take the product of the researches of other minds, but they should investigate truth for themselves," wrote Mrs. White elsewhere. "If they do not form the habit of investigating themes of truth for themselves, they will become superficial in their life and acquirements. The opinions of your associates may be of value to you, but you should not rely upon them and have no definite ideas of your own. You should examine the truths you have been led to believe, until you know they are without a flaw."[6]

But in affirming the value of intellectual inquiry, we need also to emphasize that, as Christians, our worldview is shaped by more than merely the power of human inquiry. As Ellen White expressed it, "Let the field of their study be as broad as their powers can compass; but let them make God their wisdom."[7]

The final and ultimate point of reference for the intellectual inquiries of a believer is the Word of God. However, understanding Scripture is *also* an exercise of the mind. The searching mind asks, Is there an inspired word that speaks to this issue? How should I understand it? Are there factors in the context of culture and history that are critical to a correct understanding of how God's Word speaks to the world in which I live?

2. Provide a safe harbor for the mind to search and probe. I often think of the words of one of my former teachers: "The greatest hazard to the thinking mind is the autonomy of the mind." He was saying that for an intellectually inquiring person, the greatest danger lies in attempting to resolve all questions and doubts within the privacy—and limits—of his or her own understanding. No matter how learned or how bright, no one person knows everything! It's an obvious truth, yet one we so easily forget.

The freedom of the mind must be respected and protected, yet that very freedom may take us down treacherous paths. How can we safely proceed? I've found that humility is an indispensable companion on any intellectual journey, for humility allows us to be open to the counsel and perspective of others.

When we close our minds to all but our own wisdom, we can find ourselves intellectually and spiritually unmoored. In this—as in so many other areas of the journey of faith—we must be prepared to be vulnerable, to expose our perplexity and our uncertainties, and to seek guidance and insights from those who've traveled the path before us or who are our fellow travelers.

Yet we ask too much of our young people if we expect them to be candid about their questions or doubts, but can't provide them with an intellectual safe haven. It has to do with the environment and culture we develop in our church. The youth will ask difficult questions. They need no one's permission to do that, as they frequently demonstrate. What they need is to know that their vulnerability won't be exploited and that they'll be met with openness and acceptance.

Make no mistake, no matter how strident their voices or argumentative their tone, our young people *do* feel vulnerable. Let's put aside for a moment the question of who's right and who's wrong. Their questioning may be way off. What we're talking about is the climate in which it all takes place. Making yourself vulnerable isn't an attractive option if you believe the reaction you'll receive is condemnation.

3. Provide useful tools for intellectual engagement. When I was a ten-year-old boy in northern Norway, my grandfather—not noted for his love of Adventism—confronted me with a startling question. "You Adventists," he said. "You believe that eating pork is wrong. Well, how then do you account for this?" And he showed me in Acts 10:15 where God spoke to the apostle Peter, saying, "Do not call anything impure that God has made clean" (NIV).

I was floored. I had no answer. I'd never before encountered this idea, and to see it written there in the Bible itself! It was too much for me and I found I had nothing to say.

My father helped the mind of this young boy to understand that this passage wasn't about food at all, but about mission. I suspect my grandfather knew that, but just wanted to score a point off a ten-year-old boy and do damage that's difficult to heal.

It taught me the importance of meeting young people where they are, to deal with challenges in their territory, and to resist wielding our "superior" knowledge as a tool to intimidate or silence dissent.

Where can our young people go for answers when the questions they face seem too big for them? What resources can they access? What tools do they have to negotiate through an intellectual landscape that assumes, for example, that an evolutionary explanation for human origins is the only scientifically legitimate point of view?

In 2009, staff from my office filmed a focus group at one of our church's institutions of higher learning. This was a group of four or five biology majors—scientists-in-training—each of whom had tremendous respect for the scientific method and who, at the same time, were firmly committed to their faith and church. Yet when asked to talk in depth about some of the apparent contradictions between the biblical account of Creation and what they read about in their science textbooks, they were largely at a loss for words. They tried. They theorized a little. But in essence, they said, "We don't know how to deal with this!"

How do we help them?

More than sixty years ago, the Adventist Church established the Geoscience Research Institute, in part to track developments in contemporary science and to provide a scientific perspective that was consistent with biblical truth. It does invaluable work, but is it enough? No. Providing tools to assist our young people in their journeys of discovery is a dynamic process, and there is always more we can and should do. The questions they come up with today may be different from the questions of yesterday, and what's unclear to one person may be unproblematic to another.

Teachers and parents probably carry the most significant responsibility when it comes to placing effective intellectual and spiritual tools in the hands of the young. It's a task not to be taken lightly. Our goal should be to support them in their exploration and questioning and to affirm that this is, indeed, a legitimate process. But our most important responsibility is to guide them in a way that ultimately brings them to an assurance of the power and goodness of the Almighty, whose actions we can see only "through a glass darkly." A daunting task? Perhaps, but there it is.

An often-overlooked part of our responsibility as guides for the young is to help them understand that it's OK to have some unresolved questions. A person may have worked long and earnestly with an issue; but for one reason or another, his or her mind can't find resolution. The gift of being able to let the matter rest *for now* is healthy. The journey continues, he or she grows and develops and may find that some discoveries will come in time. The person might return to a matter previously left hanging and bring to it perspectives that he or she didn't have before. The person's experiences, interactions, and new maturity may allow him or her to see what was once so elusive. In the life of the mind, nothing stands still.

Affirm the narrative of faith

A few years ago, I filmed a number of YouTube segments under the title "About Life." This was a series of short, fast-paced commentaries about key Adventist values and beliefs. One of the segments addressed the apparent clash between the world of faith and that of science, and pinpointed the danger of locking yourself into a worldview that only accepts what is empirically verifiable.

I said, "To me the world of faith is the world in which God's creative powers are constantly on display. . . . It's a world full of wonders and miracles! From the very beginning, in Genesis right through to the resurrection of Christ, to the world made new, and the resurrection of our own bodies. Miracles? For me, this is not a problem. I have them for breakfast every day!"

To be a Christian is to acknowledge the existence of a realm that exists beyond the range of normal human perception and reasoning. It's the world of God's creative powers. It's filled with wonder! This is the world of the One who will take everything we know and experience, scientific or otherwise, wrap it up, put it to the side, and say, "Behold, I make all things new."

If we don't, or can't, accept this basic premise, then what do we have left?

As young Adventists venture into difficult, sometimes frightening intellectual territory, they need an immovable anchor of faith. Our churches must be places where they see the narrative of faith at work—warm, loving, Christ centered, and mission focused.

For when our faith becomes experiential, a force that's central to our very identity, it will say to us, "Go, ask, consider, engage. But with Me to guide you,

you'll always know your way back home."

[Conversation starters]

Do you want to explore more deeply some of the issues raised in this chapter? Here are some ideas for starting a dialogue between younger and older members of your congregation.

1. **Have your say.** Have you ever gained the impression from your parents, a teacher, or others that some topics and questions are out of bounds for Seventh-day Adventists?

2. **Conversation builders.**
   - According to one Adventist writer, "Being intellectually curious—asking questions rather than accepting prepackaged answers—carries a risk of losing one's way. . . . I've always sensed, as I was launching out, that it was important to be sure I knew the way back."[8] What are some safeguards that can help protect our faith as we wrestle with difficult issues?

   - Ellen White wrote: "It is God's purpose that the kingly power of *sanctified reason,* controlled by divine grace, shall bear sway in the lives of human beings."[9] What do you think Mrs. White means by "sanctified reason"?

3. **Discussion questions.**
   - Is the response "You must have more faith!" ever a good answer to young people who are struggling with doubt? How do we affirm the vital role of faith in the life of a believer, without being dismissive of those who have questions?

   - Are there certain situations or times when it's *not* OK to ask questions— when it's more responsible to keep our intellectual struggles private?

   - If being intellectually "adventurous" brings some risk to your spiritual life, are there also dangers in being intellectually "passive"?

What now? What practical steps could you take to help make your local Adventist church or school an intellectual safe haven for young people? Are there specific safeguards you'll also need to put in place for the good of the faith community?

[Endnotes]

1. Ellen G. White, *Fundamentals of Christian Education* (Nashville, Tenn.: Southern Publishing Association, 1923), 45.

2. David Kinnaman, *You Lost Me: Why Young Christians Are Leaving Church and Rethinking Faith* (Grand Rapids, Mich.: Baker Books, 2011), 137.

3. From an interview with Christopher Hitchens on the Showtime television series *Penn & Teller: Bullshit!* season 3, episode 5: "Holier Than Thou," May 23, 2005.

4. Richard Dawkins, untitled lecture (Edinburgh Science Festival, Edinburgh, UK, 1992); quoted in Michael Ruse, *Science and Spirituality: Making Room for Faith in the Age of Science* (New York, N.Y.: Cambridge University Press, 2010), 3.

5. White, *Fundamentals of Christian Education,* 45.

6. Ellen G. White, *Counsels on Sabbath School Work* (Washington, D.C.: Review and Herald® Publishing Association, 1938), 33.

7. Ellen G. White, *Counsels to Parents, Teachers, and Students* (Mountain View, Calif.: Pacific Press® Publishing Association, 1941), 394.

8. Bert Williams, "Knowing the Way Back," *Adventist Review,* July 13, 2006, 8–11.

9. Ellen G. White, *My Life Today* (Washington, D.C.: Review and Herald®, 1952), 70; emphasis added.

Six

"Must I Be Politically Passive?"

[Faith in the World of Politics]

This is what they said

- *"Could you please clear up a disagreement between my friends and me about whether it's OK to get involved in politics? I say that Jesus was very concerned about improving the lives of the people around Him and that Christians today shouldn't be afraid to use the political system to try to do that. But according to some of my friends, when Jesus said, 'My kingdom is not of this world,' He was warning Christians to stay away from politics. Who's right?"*

- *"If I'm not mistaken, Ellen White counsels that Adventist are* not *totally prohibited from practicing the right of suffrage, but that if we vote we're indirectly responsible for the actions of the politicians we help elect. If this is true, then I'm wondering why so many Adventists in my country (where there's so much corruption in politics) are so politically engaged and outspoken."*

- *"Is there an official church stance on voting? I haven't yet voted in an election because my parents have always told me that it's best to stay out of politics. I'd like to know if it's OK to have a say in the government of your country."*

- *"I am from the Democratic Republic of Congo, although I am studying in the United States. I would very much like to pursue a career in politics because there's so much that could be done in my country. Do you think it would be wrong for me to run for elected office? Please pray for me."*

- *"I was a campaign volunteer in the last presidential election [in the United States]. I've talked to some people at church who shake their heads and warn me about the dangers of politics. Do you think there are real pitfalls in having a political opinion and acting on it?"*

- *"When youth in my church talk about getting involved in politics, the elders of the church say, 'No! You can't be an Adventist and hold political office.' But why not? I don't see anything in my Bible about that."*

- *"Neither political party reflects 100 percent my views, but I do strongly support about 75 percent of the platform of one of the parties. Would it be wrong for me to actively support my preferred party, even though they hold to a few positions that make me somewhat uncomfortable? The only other option I see is to not get involved and not to vote, and that doesn't appeal to me at all."*

- *"Is there any church guidance for people who want to take part in nonviolent civil protests and disobedience? I feel that if it's an issue of fundamental justice, then we shouldn't be scared to get involved with a civil disobedience movement to try to raise awareness about the issue. What do you think?"*

- *"I've marched in a few protests—sometimes just for the fun of it, and sometimes because I really believe in the message we're trying to send. Is there anything wrong with taking part in protests? (I'm talking here about nonviolent ones. I wouldn't want to get involved in damaging property or hurting other people.)"*

- *"I understand the concept of separation of church and state, but does that mean individual Adventists can't campaign for a candidate or even run for office ourselves? I know of a number of current and former Adventist politicians. Were they all members in good and proper standing?"*

- *"In our country, parliamentary and presidential elections are always held on Sabbath—no exceptions. Personally, I believe Christians have a responsibility to vote, so it's OK to vote on Sabbath. But I know that most of the church members here don't feel that way. Could you please send me Bible texts that could help in this situation?"*

- *"How can we make an impact on society if we don't get involved in public life? I get frustrated by people in church who act as if being politically active is sinful.*

I have strong political views, and I am very involved in supporting candidates. I do it because I think that some things in society can only be dealt with by government—or at least, the biggest impact can be made by government. Why do some Adventists seem allergic to politics? Or am I in the wrong here?"

This is what some of our young people are saying and their questions and comments are clear and well stated. What guidance can we offer?

Conflicting loyalties?

There's no ambiguity about whether the Seventh-day Adventist Church should ever meddle in partisan politics at an institutional or congregations level. The answer is "No," and there the matter rests. There's a multitude of historical, moral, and practical reasons for why this should be so—not to mention clear words of inspired counsel.[1]

Yet there seems to be less clarity when it comes to the question of how far—if at all—*individual* Adventists should be active in political issues or in the machinery of government.

"You know you're an Adventist when . . . politics is very complicated" ran an entry on the microblogging site Tumblr, posted November 5, 2012—the day before Americans went to the polls to elect a president. It continued: "As Adventists, we know that the decisions of the government can/do/will affect us, yet we know that no matter what, the End Times are gonna happen anyway. . . . Happy voting! Or not voting?"[2]

And there, in a nutshell, is the ambivalence many Adventists feel toward the political process.

The question that lies at the heart of this issue is, Can we be good citizens of God's kingdom and still be politically engaged with the "kingdoms of this world"?

Young people ask, "We want to know, because the public authorities that care for everything from sewage to welfare to education impact the lives of all people—'saints and sinners' alike. Is there any particular reason why we shouldn't contribute to that? Are secular and sacred values so hostile to each other that they can't communicate with each other? Is the separation of church and state so complete that the two must, in effect, occupy separate worlds and take care of their separate agendas?"

That's a bit unreal, isn't it?

A far-reaching message

Some years back, I visited the site of John Harvey Kellogg's Battle Creek Sanitarium in Michigan, United States. Established in 1866, it was rebuilt and expanded over the years. At its peak, the sanitarium catered to some twelve hunded patients, many of them well-known figures of the time: businessmen, politicians, scientists, entertainers, writers, and thinkers. They came to experience the revolutionary new health practices set out by Ellen White. She advocated fresh air, pure water, a plant-based diet, and exercise—concepts that were as groundbreaking then as they are conventional now.

As I walked through these massive old buildings, I was struck by the sheer audacity of our early pioneers—the enormity of their endeavor. How broad was their vision! How deep was their conviction, which drove them to such an ambitious enterprise! In these historic buildings, we can trace the roots of today's international network of Adventist hospitals, medical schools, and clinics. It was here also that the beginnings of our health food industries were nurtured and our church's medical mission work began to take shape.

It reminded me yet again that Adventism has always been concerned with the whole person. Our faith is grounded in Christ's message of wholeness—in a spiritual transformation that also encompasses the emotional and physical being. No aspect of human life lies beyond Christ's touch; no facet of human activity falls outside the scope of His care.

As Christ's followers, our interest in humanity is broad; we can't afford to arbitrarily dismiss a whole swath of human activity and say, "This is outside the scope of our concern." So perhaps when it comes to politics, the relevant question isn't "Should Adventists stay away from all things political?" but rather, "What inspired words can we find to safeguard our interactions with the political world?"

Dare to be a Daniel?

When we look to the Bible for direction, we often first go to the stories of Old Testament servants of God—Joseph, Moses, Esther, and Daniel—as prime examples of individuals who served both state and God with distinction and integrity.

I accept there may be some hints in these narratives that help us understand how we should relate to the public realm today. But we can't simply assume that God's agenda, revealed in these Old Testament stories, flows seamlessly on into contemporary society.

For a start, Israel was a theocracy, and God had specific plans for His chosen nation. He moved the activities of other nations to protect and preserve what He wanted Israel to be and to become. It's in this context that Old Testament servants of God engaged and acted.

As Paul affirms in Romans chapters 9–11, however, the cross of Christ marked an end to what had been God's plan for Israel as a nation. God chooses now a spiritual nation as His instrument of mission in the world. How can we then simply assume that the Old Testament models of political engagement by men and women of God illustrate how we should act in today's secular world? At the most, they may serve as examples of honor, ethics, integrity, and nobility of character in public service.

Called to action

As we look to the New Testament, we see Jesus telling His followers that they are to function as "light," "salt," and "yeast" in the world. He never taught, by example or saying, that His followers should distance themselves from the secular world. Why? Quite simply because it's filled with people whom Christ loves and whose well-being matters to Him!

As believers, we may long for the everlasting kingdom of God, and we may be focused on preparing ourselves and others for Christ's second coming; but for now, here we remain—living in a fundamentally broken world, surrounded by secular society and secular values.

Some young people point out to me all the corruption, greed, and power grabbing in politics and government, and ask, "Isn't that good enough reason to stay as far away as possible?" I say, "No." A Christian not only has the right but the duty to be a moral voice in society, to speak clearly and eloquently on that which touches our core values: human rights, public health, poverty, injustice, and religious freedom and tolerance—an issue particularly vital now as tension rises between the Islamic world and the West.

I think of the words of former United States president John F. Kennedy, "Never negotiate without fear; but never fear to negotiate." Yes, it's wise to step cautiously and carefully into the political realm; but take another look at Christ's words in Matthew 25. Can we doubt we have a nonnegotiable obligation to take action on behalf of people in need? Can we afford to simply ignore the role and reach of government as we pursue this mission?

A political vocation?

Some young professionals have told me they feel drawn to public service; some even feel their best contributions can be made by running for elected office. However, they don't want to be judged negatively by their church, so they ask, "Is that OK?"

The answer may well be, "Yes. If it matches your skills and sense of calling to service, then do it. But just be sure you keep your heart clean, and you don't become infected by the corruption you meet or by the fickle attraction of power."

There really is no one-size-fits-all answer for young men and women considering politics as a career. So much depends on motives, on the strength of your connection to the Lord and to your faith community, your capacity to distinguish between political compromise and personal compromise, and your ability to withstand what will surely be significant tests to your integrity.

I've known a number of Seventh-day Adventists who've served their country in high political office. Many of them have public and private records that reflect credit to their Lord and to their church. Their service has been marked by Christ-driven values of care for the vulnerable, and they've worked to enhance the quality of life for all citizens.

Some other Adventist politicians, on the other hand . . . Well, perhaps it's better to leave it there.

The passion of our early pioneers for causes such as the abolition of slavery, temperance, and religious freedom is well documented, and the counsel of Ellen White is worth remembering. "Many deplore the wrongs which they know exist, but consider themselves free from all responsibility in the matter," she wrote in 1914. "This cannot be. Every individual exerts an influence in society."[3]

In an earlier statement addressing teachers and students in Battle Creek, Michigan, in 1883, Mrs. White said, "Have you thoughts that you dare not express, that you may one day . . . sit in deliberative and legislative councils, and help to enact laws for the nation? There is nothing wrong in these aspirations."[4]

The inspired counsel is clear. Opting out of public concerns isn't a legitimate Christian option. Just make sure that if you're a political office holder serving a secular city, state, or nation, you never compromise your Christian values. Your first loyalty is always to Christ.

To vote or not to vote? It's personal.

For every Seventh-day Adventist who actually runs for public office, however, there are hundreds of thousands whose only political engagement is voting in an election. (I'm speaking here, of course, about those who live in countries ruled by democratic principles.)

Yet, even here, there's confusion. The questions I received through *Let's Talk* show that a great many of our young people are unsure how their faith should guide them in exercising their rights as a citizen.

"Is promoting one political party, taking part in its rallies, and pushing one particular candidate in preference to another an acceptable activity for me as a church member?" they asked. "If my candidate is elected, do I become in some way responsible or accountable for that person's ethical and moral behavior once in office?"

The answers aren't simple because each one of us has to make our own judgment call based on the best information we can find. You may well be criticized for your decision, but so be it! If you're going to run away from everything that may attract criticism, you probably won't accomplish anything worthwhile in life.

Keep in mind as you take part in the political process that candidates sometimes have a remarkable ability to transform themselves once they're elected. Values candidates passionately supported in the election campaign may all but disappear once the newly minted leaders start exercising official power. You may have supported the candidates at some stage in their pursuit of office, but this doesn't make you accountable for the decisions they make later. They're exercising their own free choice, over which you have no control. There's no remedy—except to vote them out when their term is up.

The Adventist Church has never made an across-the-board ruling about political involvement, and it never should. We each have to think, pray, and examine our hearts. It's not easy to make the right call at times, and we may well make mistakes. But remember, as followers of Christ we can't walk away from our communities. We have a responsibility to do all we can to make our city, province, and/or nation a safer, kinder, healthier place to live for everyone—especially for the most vulnerable among us. This, also, is what it means to be a Christian.

[Conversation starters]

Do you want to explore more deeply some of the issues raised in this chapter? Here are some ideas for starting a dialogue between younger and older members of your congregation.

1. Have your say. As Seventh-day Adventists, we identify ourselves as a "peculiar people" with a specific end-time message. How do you respond to the suggestion that political involvement is a distraction that draws time and energy away from our true mission?

2. Conversation builders.
- New Testament writers often describe God's people as "strangers" or "foreigners" on the earth, whose true citizenship is in heaven. (See, for example, 1 Peter 2:10; Hebrews 11:13; Philippians 3:20.) Because our citizenship lies elsewhere, could this mean we should keep our distance from the political concerns of our community or nation?

- Jane Sabes, a political science professor at Andrews University, writes that when Adventists stay away from politics, "public policy is left to unbelievers: School curriculum is designed, national policy is set, and global determinations are made without offering a Christian, a Seventh-day Adventist perspective."[5] Why should (or shouldn't!) we be concerned about this?

3. Discussion questions.
- Imagine the day-to-day life of an Adventist who holds political office. In what ways would his or her principles be tested? Is compromise inevitable?

- Do Adventist values and beliefs have anything significant to contribute to current political debates? Can you think of any public policy issues in today's headlines where an Adventist perspective could be valuable?

What now? Does our church clearly explain to young people the difference between healthy civic participation and unhealthy political partisanship? Could your local congregation do more to provide such guidance *without* stepping into the realm of partisan politics?

[Endnotes]

1. While affirming the right of individual Adventists to vote, Ellen White also wrote: "We are not as a people to become mixed up with political questions." *Selected Messages,* 2:336, 337.

2. You Know You're Adventist . . . , accessed November 25, 2012, http://yeahadventists.tumblr .com/.

3. Ellen G. White, "The Temperance Work," *Review and Herald,* October 15, 1914.

4. White, *Fundamentals of Christian Education,* 82.

5. Jane Sabes, "Is There a Role for Adventists in Politics?" *College and University Dialogue* 18, no. 3 (2006): 8.

Seven

"Can I Serve My Country Too?"

[Adventists and the Military]

This is what they said

- *"Obviously, I don't believe murder is right, but killing isn't always murder. The commandment against murder doesn't mean that Christians can't kill in some circumstances. What about self-defense? What about the responsibility of the strong to watch out for the weak? Take the Second World War, for example. Were we going to let Hitler trample over helpless countries and simply let him try to exterminate all the Jews? So if we as Adventists won't fight, that means we have to let others in our country fight on our behalf. We say, 'Let the Baptists fight the war,' or 'The Lutherans can take care of it.' I guess what I'm saying is that although war is a terrible thing, and often brings atrocities on both sides, Christians can and should sometimes fight in wars."*

- *"I have a once-in-a-lifetime chance to work in a weapons defense systems program. It's programming computers and is something that would really draw on my training and skills. But I'm not sure what God wants me to do. Our country needs to defend itself, so is working on a military defense system really that bad?"*

- *"I really want to join the army and my parents are OK with that—they're happy that I'll be getting a college education at the same time. Some of my friends say that the church teaches that we shouldn't join the military. What are the wrongs and rights of this?"*

- *"I'm thinking of joining the military and would like to work in Air Force intelligence. There are a lot of opportunities that don't involve actual combat, so it's not like I would be on the front lines. In fact, I think this area has more to do with defense of our country than anything else. Do you think God would mind someone doing that?"*

- *"Is there any such thing as a 'just war' and does our church ever weigh in on conflicts around the world? My father says that the Second World War was clearly a case of a just war. If that's the case, wouldn't it follow that we would not only have the right but the responsibility to take an active part in the military? Why then does our church have a blanket position against joining the military?"*

- *"Will I be disfellowshiped if I perform my national service requirement? I will have to train with and carry weapons."*

- *"I have friends who serve in the military, and I'm proud of what they're doing and thankful for their sacrifice on behalf of everyone else. I think we need to do more to acknowledge that and not make them feel like they're betraying their faith. They are doing a necessary and honorable job."*

- *"I read about church members in South Korea who go to prison rather than carry arms as part of their national service. Why do Adventists in some parts of the world take this so seriously, while in other countries military service is seen as OK (or at least isn't discouraged)?"*

- *"I'm uncomfortable when people in my church talk about 'our men and women in uniform' or ask for prayers for 'our troops' fighting overseas. I hear this a lot. Do you think that this belongs in church?"*

- *"This may be a strange question, but has the church changed its position on noncombatancy? The reason I ask is that no one ever talks about it. I've read a number of books about Adventist Church members long ago who refused to fight. So, what's our teaching today? And if it's different to what we taught in the past, why [and] how did this come about? Thanks."*

- *"War is a fact of today's world, so why doesn't our church have more to say about international issues of war and peace? Are we so totally inward looking that we can afford to pretend that this is none of our business? It seems to me that war is a moral issue, and if the church wants to be taken seriously, we should have something to say about this!"*

- *"I find it disturbing that we are so far from our past as noncombatants. This used to be one of our 'distinctive' teachings, but we're pretty much silent on it now at the very time when people need some clarity."*

These are the issues that some of our young people are struggling to resolve. Can we help them?

Moral dilemmas we can't avoid

The questions come from every possible angle: Is there such a thing as "a just war"? Is there a difference between killing and murder? What's wrong with expressing your patriotism and loyalty to your country by joining the army? Should we be praying for "our men and women in uniform" in our churches? Have we changed our historic position on noncombatancy? Why don't we speak more about war and peace?

Every morning we wake up, there's a war raging somewhere. Around the world, the machinery of war brutally kills not just members of the military but innocent men, women, and children as well. And much of it is done in the name of patriotism and loyalty to country. Clearly, something is fundamentally wrong.

In many ways I'm a child of the Second World War. As a young boy I saw the terrible destruction to lives, families, and societies inflicted by war. My family had evacuated to the countryside, and for the five years of the war we lived in the caretaker's flat of an old school building. The classrooms had been turned into dormitories that housed more than three hundred young German soldiers.

I remember one day toward the end of the war asking my mother, "Why are the German soldiers crying?" I could hear them sobbing in their rooms. My mother replied, "They are just young boys. They miss their home; they miss their mommies and daddies. They don't understand why they have to be here in the cold of northern Norway. They don't understand why they have to be a part of all this." They were young men, deprived of the chance to grow up and experience a youth of a different kind.

Today, many years removed from that time, the world has undergone profound changes—political, economic, and technological. Yet the role of the military in the life of many nations, as well as in transnational disputes around the globe, continues to place firmly before us an important moral and spiritual question, How should Christians—Seventh-day Adventist Christians—relate to the military? And when faced with a choice to serve in the armed forces, either as a combatant or in some other capacity, what principles should direct us?

Essential guideposts

We each feel strong kinship—a sense of solidarity—with our own people and our own country. Our citizenship in a nation commands a sense of loyalty, a sharing in both the struggles and the joys of the people among whom we live. It's natural to feel civic pride. Yet how should this sense of solidarity express itself when it comes to the military of our country, when our paramount duty to God raises tensions that aren't always easy to reconcile?

I believe any discussion of this topic must rest on two essential foundations.

First, *the church is called to be an unambiguous voice of principle.*

War, peace, and participation in military service are not morally neutral issues. Scripture is not silent on these things, and the church, as it interprets and expresses the principles of Scripture, must be a voice of moral authority and influence. This is not an optional responsibility—one that we can put aside should it become uncomfortable or go against majority feeling. If we're silent, we fail in our duty to God and to humanity.

Second, *the church is God's agent of grace.*

This, also, is a fundamental responsibility. Every human being, no matter what his or her choices or conduct, is of infinite value to God. As the church expresses itself on this issue and offers counsel to both its own members and broader society, it must never allow itself to forget this one unchangeable fact: the God we serve is a Healer and a Savior. Healing and saving are also the first business of the church. As individuals struggle with these questions—and perhaps make choices that, in hindsight, they wish they hadn't—the church must constantly reflect God's infinite, healing love.

So, keeping these things in mind, I'd like to reflect on two questions regarding the church's attitude toward military service, both historically and today. These questions—broad areas of concerns—have come to me time and again over recent years, especially as I've talked with our young people, for whom these questions have very real and serious consequences.

A loss of clarity?

The historic position of our church regarding service in the armed forces was clearly expressed some 150 years ago—very early on in our history, against the background of the American Civil War. The consensus, expressed in articles and documents of the time, as well as an 1867 General Conference resolution, was unequivocal. "[T]he bearing of arms, or engaging in war, is a direct violation of the teachings of our Savior and the spirit and letter of the law of God."[1] This has, in broad terms, been our guiding principle: when you carry arms, you imply that you are prepared to use them to take another's life, and taking the life of one of God's children, even that of our "enemy," is inconsistent with what we hold to be sacred and right. Through the years, this principle has shaped the conduct of Adventists both in times of peace and conflict. Many have chosen to engage in medical work within the armed forces. They participate as healers. They say to their nation: "I can't operate as a taker of life; it would destroy me as an individual. But I can help people who are hurt by this conflict. I can function as a Christian if I can function as a healer."

Today, in some countries young people are subject to a draft—a period of compulsory military service. Fortunately, in most instances an alternate service is offered, one that doesn't require an individual to train with or use arms. This option could simply be spending a year and a half doing hard labor building roads or helping with some other civic project.

There are, however, some countries where the draft deprives you of the ability to conduct yourself as an Adventist believer. You can't keep the Sabbath. You're given no option but to carry arms. In such circumstances, you have before you a very serious choice. Accepting the penalty of dissent—perhaps even imprisonment—may be the decision you make simply to be faithful to your fundamental convictions and your Lord.

Is there any confusion today about the church's position? Have we done a good job of articulating these principles? Clearly, this question will not be answered in the same way in every part of the world church. Yet, I have sensed at times a certain ambivalence toward our historic position—a feeling, perhaps, that "that was then, and this is now." And yet I know of no reason why this should be so.

A lack of moral guidance?

This leads me to my second question. Do we provide adequate guidance in our churches and schools for our young people as they face difficult choices regarding service in the military? Have we neglected our role as a moral compass on this issue? In the absence of guidance from their churches, do some of our young people view joining the military as just another career option, rather than a complex moral decision with potentially far-reaching, maybe unforeseen, consequences for their own spiritual lives?

It's not difficult to understand the forces that may lead people to consider military careers. Their choice may be driven by a desire to serve their country, or the military may open up educational and professional opportunities that may seem unavailable anywhere else. Young people may see it as a short-term option, a much-needed stepping-stone to something else. They may view it as a necessary evil—a road to the future that, for lack of financial resources or other opportunities, they must take in order to fulfill their potential.

Yet, in some instances, to voluntarily enlist in the armed forces is to sacrifice one's choice not to bear arms or to request provision for Sabbath keeping. You freely choose to give up your rights in these things. And so I would ask, "Have you really thought about this? Have you considered the consequences to your relationship with Christ and to your own deepest convictions?"

Some may calculate the risk and say, "Although I technically don't have a choice about whether or not I will carry arms, the chances are, nine out of ten, that I will not find myself in a combat situation where I will need to use them."

But regardless of whether you go into combat or not, you have made a decision about certain basic values and declared this publicly. You are accepting the possibility that you may have to go down that road, and this will inevitably do something to you as a person. It will change and shape you. In proactively choosing to accept circumstances where you may be required to carry arms or forfeit your ability to keep the Sabbath, I suggest that you have placed the spiritual and moral foundations of your life in serious jeopardy.

So, when military recruiters come to our universities and colleges, or even our secondary schools, laying out before young students the opportunities that the armed forces present, is the church providing a clear alternate message? Is there someone also asking, "Have you considered this? Have you thought about what this may do to you? Have you thought about the price you may pay in terms of the basic values you really treasure?"

I feel especially for those young people who have taken the calculated risk and find themselves drawn into combat situations, the very positions they'd hoped and prayed to avoid. They see no way out. What should their church say to them? "I told you so?" "Shame on you?" No! The church is a ministering, healing, saving community. This is the moment when young people, regardless of poor choices or wrong turns, need to feel the embrace of their church.

No easy answers

This is not a simple topic, nor is it complete; it's just one aspect of the broader issue of war, peace, and Christian responsibility. And the questions I've posed don't lend themselves to sound-bite answers or pat responses. They're questions that generate strong—sometimes visceral—feelings. They reach deep into our self-understanding and identity as both citizens of our country and members of God's family. Our responses are shaped in large part by our own experiences and culture as well as our love for our country and our desire to share in its history and future.

Although these are difficult issues, they can't be put aside simply for this reason. We owe it to our young people to keep considering these things together—in our homes, our churches, and our schools—and to do so with open hearts and a spirit of humility.

[Conversation starters]

Do you want to explore more deeply some of the issues raised in this chapter? Here are some ideas for starting a dialogue between younger and older members of your congregation.

1. **Have your say.** Jesus often urged a nonviolent response to evil. (Read Matthew 5:9, 38, 39, 43–48, and Luke 6:27, 28.) In light of these passages, do you think we can ever justify direct involvement in military action?

2. **Conversation builders.**

    *   Gary Councell, Chaplaincy Ministries director for the General Conference, worries that Adventist young adults "no longer wrestle with the ethics of military service," and may view it as a career decision rather than a moral question.[2] What are some of these moral issues that young people may face in volunteering for military service?

    *   For some, joining the armed forces offers an education, a career, or even an escape from poverty. Are these legitimate considerations in weighing the moral implications of military service?

3. **Discussion questions.**

    *   In a time of war, don't Adventists have a duty to support their nation?

    *   Is it possible for a congregation to affirm the courage or sacrifice of church members who serve in the military (by honoring them in a special church service, for instance), without necessarily endorsing their decisions to carry arms or to become a part of the military machine?

What now? Has the Adventist Church generally done a good or poor job of explaining its position on noncombatancy? What are two or three practical ways that your local church could provide better guidance to young people on this issue?

[Endnotes]

1. Fifth Annual General Conference Session, 1867, General Conference Archives: 29—GCS, 63–88.

2. Quoted in Elizabeth Lechleitner, "Young Adventists in a World of War," *Adventist Review,* June 14, 2007, accessed December 2, 2012, http://www.adventistreview.org/article/1191/archives /issue-2007-1516/young-adventists-in-a-world-of-war.

Eight

"Modern-Day Pharisees?"

This is what they said

- *"I would like to suggest to the president that our focus needs to be on people and how we treat them. For too long, our church has focused on rules and regulations—jewelry, makeup, what you can and cannot use in church for instruments of praise, whether someone drinks or smokes or orders their pizza with pepperoni. You get the idea. These issues all have their place, but abiding by the rules has become more important in our church than how we treat others. We've become modern-day Pharisees."*

- *"Every time I mention to someone that I am a Seventh-day Adventist, I almost always get one of these responses: 'Oh, you're the ones that don't drink coffee or anything with caffeine in it.' 'You're the ones that are mostly vegetarian or vegan, right?' 'Adventist, you say? You don't drink any type of alcohol do you?' For once, I would like to be known for how gracious and accepting we are of others, or how we model ourselves after Christ, or how we don't judge others in our church, instead of being known for how we restrict our diets or for what we consider to be healthy or unhealthy."*

- *"Here's the problem with how the church talks to young people about standards and making choices about entertainment, jewelry, and what we eat and drink: It drums the 'Adventist behavior formula' into you, but as you get older, a lot of it doesn't make sense. So then you have two choices—either you throw the whole thing out, or you become a hypocrite; put on a good front whenever you need to, and do what you want the rest of the time."*

Music and worship

- *"We're in a bit of a fix here and need some advice. Last Sabbath, I led the singing at the start of the service. On Monday, I got hauled into the pastor's office and told that this praise singing had caused a lot of calls of complaint. Even though the only accompaniment was a piano, apparently the songs had 'too much tempo' and 'too much emotion.' Young people here are longing for an outlet for worship that's relevant to them. How do we resolve this dispute with our pastoral team?"*

- *"Is it right to play drums during the church service on the Sabbath day, or any other worship time in the church? If it is right, then please explain why. And if it is wrong, then please explain why. This question is causing arguments between me and my friends and the elders and pastor of the church I attend. Please, seriously, we need help."*

- *"I'm from Zimbabwe and I would like to know what you can do to ensure that young people are free to worship God in a truly fulfilling way, especially through music, when our parents and elders do not appreciate the music we favor. The situation is so discouraging to our youth."*

- *"Why do we act as if the only worship that's acceptable is 'sedated worship'? Aren't we supposed to be happy about the good news of Christ's second coming? Aren't we supposed to make a joyful noise unto the Lord? So why aren't we doing it? I've been in churches where if the singing or praise level rose above a certain decibel, people turned and stared as though it was wrong."*

- *"It's my dream of one day becoming a musician. But the thing is, I'm not sure that I want to sing gospel music. I don't want to sing music that talks about sex, drugs, and things like that. I just don't want to sing gospel music. Do you see a problem with that?"*

- *"There are a lot of issues and concerns going around at the moment about true worship and music, especially in my church in England. Where can I go to find out how Adventists are truly supposed to worship?"*

- *"Here in Mexico, drums are banned in church. But I've seen that in many parts of the world, that's not the case. I even saw on Hope TV at the GC session in St. Louis there was a set of drums on stage! Why are other Seventh-day Adventists around the world allowed to play contemporary Christian music and we're restricted to mostly old hymns played with piano?"*

Appearance

- *"As Adventists, we don't believe in wearing jewelry, right? So how do we explain Ezekiel 16:11–14 where the Lord declares, 'I adorned you with jewelry: I put bracelets on your arms and a necklace around your neck, and I put a ring on your nose, earrings on your ears and a beautiful crown on your head' [NIV]?"*

- *"My cousin recently got married and the pastor got into a tizzy because some of the bridal party were wearing jewelry, and he wouldn't let them participate unless they took it off (they weren't Adventist). Wouldn't Jesus have accepted them with open arms, earrings or no earrings? The pastor told them that they could wear earrings outside the church but not inside! Isn't that downright hypocrisy?"*

- *"Adults tell us we're not allowed to wear jewelry because we could use the money for something else that's useful. But what about the people who buy expensive clothes? But I think the same argument could be made about all the adults who are wearing designer-label clothes."*

- *"Do you consider it a sin to wear jewelry or makeup? The argument that we shouldn't spend too much time focused on onward appearance doesn't hold water. Just take a look around the church, and you'll see that women (and men!) are obviously focusing time, attention, and money on their appearance in other ways. Isn't it fair to say that it's not a problem if jewelry and makeup are used in moderation, and if more focus is placed on the inner self than the outer self? I'm not trying to be rebellious, I just need to know why I should or shouldn't do certain things. I want to know for myself, not just blindly do what people tell me."*

- *"I'm from Trinidad, and here we're not allowed to wear any makeup such as lipstick or nail polish. In the satellite evangelism series that was aired last year, and in other programs, I've seen many people participating who were wearing makeup. Answer me this: why were these sisters wearing makeup? And they are still Seventh-day Adventist?"*

- *"Aren't standards in the Seventh-day Adventist Church supposed to be the same across the country and around the world, regardless of culture and tradition?*

Why do we differ so much in regards to the dos and don'ts, like dress, earrings, short skirts, Sabbath keeping, women wearing trousers in church? It doesn't make sense."

Health message

- *"Are we really still teaching that some meats have satanic properties? I believe in healthy eating, and I believe that pork is overall a fairly unhealthy meat. But I would never assign to it the word* abomination. *I was raised an 'unclean-food-abstinent Adventist,' and as a result when I've eaten at other people's homes I've gone hungry and made my hosts feel guilty more than a few times. Then I came across verses such as Mark 7:19 and 1 Corinthians 10:25. How long will we tell people that God won't like them if they eat certain foods?"*

- *"OK, I know that getting drunk is bad. However, what about drinking one glass of wine at your sister's wedding? Is that a sin?"*

- *"How do I convince someone that drinking alcohol is wrong when Jesus did that whole water-into-wine miracle and when there are so many studies that say a moderate amount of wine is good for your health? I am very confused."*

- *"The problem is that we [young people] live in the real world, and in the real world decisions about drinking or not drinking alcohol, eating meat or being a vegetarian are not religious choices; they're lifestyle or health choices. I think it's a mistake to try to make these religious tests. That approach doesn't hang together."*

Entertainment

- *"I'm concerned about the all or nothing approach to dancing. I have been to Jewish and Greek weddings where the dance was cultural, not at all sexually provocative, and it appeared to me that this was the type of dance probably done by Miriam in the Old Testament. Many children are taught folk dance in school. Are we throwing this out as well?"*

- *"I was wondering, a lot of people in my church say dancing is wrong. I don't understand why. I've never found anything in the Bible that says dancing is wrong. Could you explain to me?"*

- *"We are told that 'angels do not enter theaters.' When it comes to movies, our church's emphasis is not on what we're viewing but the place where we're viewing it! We need to be taught how to discern between wholesome entertainment and what's displeasing to God. Focusing on 'place' rather than on 'content' is ridiculous, and young people know it. It has no credibility."*

- *"What's wrong with going to the movie theater? I would think that the problem should be the movie and not the place itself. I've read what's in the church manual, but it's so vague. Could you shed some light on this for me? Thanks."*

- *"I know most of my Adventist friends go to the movies, but my parents say I shouldn't go. However, I think it's alright to go to the movies, so long as the show is OK. My question is: Are Seventh-day Adventists allowed to go to the movies? Or are my parents right?"*

This is what our young people are saying to their church, and they're fair comments. What do we say in response?

Choosing from society's buffet

From the perspective of later years, it can be difficult to remember the intensity—and perplexity—with which we once contemplated the vast array of choices that confronted us as we entered the adult world. Perhaps some older people listened to the *Let's Talk* conversations and said, "Why is he wasting time having these unnecessary discussions? Can't he simply tell them how it should be, down the line, very sharply?"

But the sheer volume and variety of questions about Christian behavior I received throughout the seven-year life of *Let's Talk* reveal that some of our young people are genuinely struggling. What should they wear, what activities are OK, where should or shouldn't they go, what shouldn't they be listening to or watching?

The questions I encountered ranged from the trivial to those of considerable depth and significance. At times it would have been easy to offer a dismissive response, "You know, this issue has been covered before . . . more than once." But then, I'd remember that these young men and women weren't being prompted by a mere academic interest in the subject. They were asking because the question related to their real lives—what had happened to them last week, a decision they made yesterday, or plans they have with their friends for Saturday night. For them, this is the stuff of everyday reality in a media-saturated world that seems to offer them an endless array of possibilities and choices.

The problem of "maybe"

Some young people asked their questions with embarrassment; others, with defiance. Some said, "I have friends I hang out with—they're not Adventists—and you know, sometimes I'm not sure what I should say to them about these things." Or some young professionals said, "In my work life, I'm drawn into an 'interesting' range of social situations—and things happen. I feel compromised. I don't quite know how to handle this."

Yet underlying each question was an appeal: "I'm genuinely conflicted about something that's important to me, and I'm coming to you, someone I see as a custodian of church values, and asking you to clear up my confusion."

Except I couldn't—or at least not in the way they perhaps expected or hoped. I found as I talked with young people about these things that they often found principle-based responses very unsatisfying. They wanted the "yes or no" answer, not the "maybe" answer.

As a young man, I didn't much like ambiguity either when it came to questions of behavior. Either something was right or it was wrong; black was black, white was white. It was obvious!

Yet with years and maturity came a clearer sense of the danger of teaching Christian standards in a way that bypasses the reasoning process.

Braided hair, music choices, clothing, makeup—do we really think we can find answers that will apply universally?

How then do we guide our young people?

Let's go to the points they raise.

"Is living with rules a type of modern-day Phariseeism?"

All groups that live together in some kind of community, whether large or small—village, city, or nation—are surrounded by accepted norms and laws governing day-to-day life. This is basic to living together as human beings. There are rights and wrongs—behavioral conventions—that build and strengthen groups, and without them would come anarchy and chaos. This is how it is, and it's not a particularly Christian innovation. Living with standards and rules in society really needs no defense; the absence of these leaves us defenseless and vulnerable. And it's no less true for a believer living with Christian values and norms.

Owning our principles

To young people who say Adventism is weighed down in the eyes of the public with too many behavior-related constraints, I'd say, "Why should it be embarrassing to be known for our robust Christian values and high standards for behavior? Instead, look at it as the quality of life you've chosen. You've taken this path because it has value to you. If you've made this decision intelligently and rationally, it should be something you feel good about because it's *you*. It's an essential expression of your identity."

But, they may respond, isn't focusing on behavior just too negative?

There's no inherent conflict between holding high standards for our behavior and being gracious people, who accept others and extend Christ's love to everyone. I can be a vegetarian and have good times with others who don't share my dietary habits. I won't be uncomfortable in their company, and I'll do my best to make sure they're not uncomfortable in mine. Even in the privacy of my mind, I'll resist judging them simply because they're different in some ways from me. That, I think, is Christ's model.

Living our principles

As a young graduate student at a large secular university in Europe, I was often invited with my wife, Kari, to social events with other members of my study group. They knew us well as Seventh-day Adventists, and we knew them. They often served wine, but they provided other choices for us. It didn't embarrass us or the host. We'd made it known that this was simply the way we were, the others accepted our choice, and together we relaxed and had many good times.

Do rules and standards of themselves make a person hypocritical or Pharisaical? No, not unless they're false fronts, erected for public appearances, that don't genuinely reflect what we are or what we carry in our hearts. If that's so, then you're a fake: your social life will become a problem, and you'll become a problem to yourself. Something has to give, for no one can live a double life indefinitely.

How can we deal with music and worship?

Just how big a role does music play in the life of teens and young adults?

According to a recent study in the United States, the average time young people listen to music each day has been steadily increasing for more than a decade, and now hovers around the two-hour-and-twenty-minute mark.[1] No doubt this trend has been fed by music downloading and sharing Web sites, along with rapid changes in technology that have made music so portable. But sociologists tell us that music has long been a pervasive force within youth culture, playing a massive role in how many young people shape and express their developing sense of identity.[2]

Are we surprised then that music in worship can become such a contentious issue within our congregations? It surfaced as a problem area in every single *Let's Talk* television broadcast and generated a steady flow of comments and questions through the Let's Talk Web site. Our young people left me in no doubt that the generational and cultural gaps were huge on this issue, and that they felt precise standards were lacking.

An all-purpose approach?

Our young people want consistency in both standards and how we apply them. They say, "We're a global church with shared faith values around the world. Regardless of whether you come from Asia, Africa, Latin America, or Europe, being a Seventh-day Adventists basically means the same thing. Couldn't we have the same music standards everywhere?"

And my answer to that is both "Yes" and "No."

"Yes" in that music in worship, in any culture, must be worshipful. Music must be a means by which we, as part of a congregation, turn to God in adoration and worship (as do the angelic choirs in Revelation), acknowledging Him as Creator, confessing our shortcomings, and acknowledging God's incredible gift of salvation in Jesus Christ. Our music must communicate hope and allow the believer to reach out with longing for the return of our Lord and the eternal future He'll bring. Music in worship is both personal and communal—it's the confession of each individual believer as well the congregation as a whole. It helps bind the community of believers together as a family.

"Yes" to all of that.

But "No" to uniformity. Music, in and out of church, is so much a product of culture. Musical instruments considered appropriate for worship will vary: some types of drums may work well in parts of the Caribbean and Africa, but they'd be considered most unsuitable for community worship in other cultures. This shouldn't surprise anyone. There will be differences around the world, for we are all children of our own cultures. It's not a good idea to be overly opinionated about what's suitable in a culture other than one's own, nor should we be too hasty in importing worship music from one culture to another.

Are there some songs or styles of music that are unsuitable in any culture? Yes, I think so. Let me suggest just two.

- Songs with dubious lyrics that contain no recognizable tribute to God, or with endless repetition of a few words or phrases that leave the mind essentially empty. (I call these "seven-eleven songs"—meaning seven words, repeated eleven times.) Perhaps at times these songs also have a rhythm that attempts to compensate for the low thought content.

- Secular pop music that's been lightly "baptized" (or maybe just "sprinkled") with some religious words tossed into the mix. This is music from another world, not born in a spiritual setting, and has little or nothing to contribute to the worship of God. In fact, it may do the opposite, drawing one away from God toward the secular world that gave it life.

Are we still hung up on appearance?

Often I was asked by a young woman or young man, Is wearing (some article of clothing or jewelry or makeup or hairstyle) a sin?

As with music, culture is tremendously important in setting the context for any discussion about appearance. So the relevant question is probably not, "Is this a sin?" but rather, "Is it appropriate for me as a Seventh-day Adventist living in the culture where I am? Is it in bad taste? Would it be offensive to my community of faith?"

As General Conference president, I visited a different congregation almost every Sabbath, often traveling to different countries from week to week. I can confirm from firsthand observation that we don't all dress the same, and sometimes the standards of what's considered acceptable vary hugely. And that's OK. We live where we live. Everyone should feel comfortable that they're representing Christ and their church aright within their particular environments. We should feel comfortable; we should feel that we're *dressed appropriately for the occasion.*

And that standard, by its very nature, is tremendously subjective.

I believe lists of approved items or styles intended for global church use are an offensive intrusion into people's own spaces and a degrading imposition on their right—indeed, responsibility—to keep their personal choices in harmony with their spiritual values.

Yes, we've always advocated modesty, and we've drawn from Scripture the principle that beauty is something you *are,* not something you apply to your face or hang on your body.

It would be a grave mistake, however, for any of us to look at a person's appearance and begin to have opinions about his or her spiritual life. We're so prone to do that and we forget that Christ examines the heart.

Can I eat that?

I was stuck by one question I received: "Are we really still teaching that some meats have satanic properties?"

Have we ever taught that? I don't think so. So how could this young person have absorbed such an idea?

To focus our health message around two or three big issues is to caricature healthful living. A healthful lifestyle is broad and comprehensive, and it has as much to do with exercise and rest, clean water and sunshine, and a healthy attitude, as it has to do with what's on our plate.

But eating and drinking *is* part of the equation. Maybe the right question to ask is, "Does it matter to God what we eat and drink, or is that somehow too trivial to occupy His thoughts?"

Through the apostle Paul, God has said that our bodies are the temple of the Holy Spirit (1 Corinthians 6:19). Ellen White writes that our intellectual, moral, and spiritual vigor are tied to our physical health.[3] We live only as a *whole* person, and all of our faculties touch each other.

So, yes, it matters what we eat and drink. In fact, these choices will often have an influence on our choices in other areas of our life. When it comes to alcohol, especially, our social lives will be significantly shaped by our choices. It seems clear that when we talk about living strong and healthy lives, functioning effectively for God, and honoring the One who made us individually "temples of the Holy Spirit," then we can't ignore what we put into our bodies. It's too big a part of our lives to be declared nonessential.

You can't divide your life into segments. You can't draw a line around the religious part of your person and behavior, and set it apart from everything else. If you're a believer, then which part of your personal life is excluded from that?

"It's just one glass"

"What's wrong with one glass of wine occasionally?" some young people ask. A lot. First, research and statistics quickly dispel the notion that there's such a thing as "one glass" of wine. There are usually many more as the proverbial "just one glass" picks up other baggage along the way. Before you know it, alcohol has become a part of your life and is shaping your social life and choice of friends. Its potential to destroy your health, your family life, and yes, your spiritual life, shouldn't be taken lightly.

Indulging in "just one glass" represents a dangerous step away from the holistic, balanced approach to healthy living that our church advocates.

Are we "allowed" to?

It worries me when I hear so many of our young people prefacing their questions with "Are we, as Seventh-day Adventists, allowed to . . . ?" Whether the question is about food, drink, jewelry, movies or dancing, the word *allowed* sounds a troubling note.

The answer is, Well, yes, as an autonomous human being endowed by God with reason and freedom of choice, you are "allowed" to do whatever it is you're contemplating. It's your choice, whether it's wise or not.

The Adventist Church is a community of volunteers. Being part of our faith community is a choice people have freely made, in part because of the quality of life and values they find here. This is what they want!

It works the same way within a family. At an early age, the term "allowed to" is a valuable and important instrument for teaching children values. But as a child moves through adolescence and their teen years, a different approach must gradually come into play, or the parents' influence will decline—rapidly.

Yes, there are standards which, in part, express our identity, but there's no grand cross-cultural Adventist rulebook that dictates behavior every step of the way. People have to make choices, and these must make sense—be owned—by the individual who is doing the choosing.

Our intellect, guided by spiritual and moral values and turned prayerfully toward God, must be constantly engaged. And the choices I make must be *mine;* they must reflect what I think is proper Christian behavior within the time and culture where I live. If I don't own my choices, the Christian walk becomes joyless, focused around a series of cumbersome chores that, sooner or later, I'll probably just set aside.

Clearly, we'll never fully settle certain questions about Christian behavior and standards. These issues will keep reappearing as each new generation wrestles with the moral and spiritual implications of making personal choices. The questions will keep coming up, also, because they relate to the stuff of everyday life—and behavior can be very visible in the life of a faith community.

To those of us of the older generation who, whether we know it or not, wield such tremendous influence over young people, both positive and destructive, I'd simply say: "Look, these are our children, and they're seeking a legitimate identity for themselves within the church. Help them find it. Don't drive them away. Rather, let's do all we can to help them understand the trust and also the responsibility that is theirs."

[Conversation starters]

Do you want to explore more deeply some of the issues raised in this chapter? Here are some ideas for starting a dialogue between younger and older members of your congregation.

1. **Have your say.** Do Seventh-day Adventist young people need *more* or *less* guidance from their church on issues such as clothing and appearance, eating and drinking, or entertainment choices?

2. **Conversation builders.**
   - In Matthew 23, Jesus condemns the legalism and hypocrisy of the Pharisees, who focused on behavior while neglecting "justice, mercy and faithfulness" (verse 23, NIV). Yet in Matthew 5:20, Jesus says, "Unless your righteousness surpasses that of the Pharisees . . . you will certainly not enter the kingdom of heaven" (NIV). Will focusing on behavior always lead to legalism? Or is Jesus' message more nuanced?

   - Historian Christine King says some Adventists in Germany during the pre-war years welcomed Hitler's rise to power, in part because they related to "his abstinence from tea, coffee, alcohol and meat."[4] Clearly, judging others by certain benchmarks of behavior is dangerous. But is it sometimes OK, or even necessary? What about someone who's going astray and needs guidance?

3. **Discussion questions.**
   - Should a congregation ever look at a general principle of Christian behavior, such as dressing in a modest way, and produce a specific list of what's acceptable or not?

   - How would your congregation react if a member of your youth group arrived at church one Sabbath morning with a tattoo or piercing?

   - Is there a clear way of distinguishing between standards that apply to all people, everywhere and those that are dependent on culture?

What now? Sometimes young people feel picked on or judged when older people talk to them about their personal choices. What could your congregation do to nurture a healthier cross-generational dialogue about Christian behavior and standards?

[Endnotes]

1. Victoria J. Rideout, Ulla G. Foehr, and Donald F. Roberts, eds., *Generation M2: Media in the Lives of 8-18 Year Olds: A Kaiser Family Foundation Study* (Menlo Park, Calif.: Henry J. Kaiser Family Foundation, 2010), 28.

2. See, for instance, Dan Laughey, *Music and Youth Culture* (Edinburgh, UK: Edinburgh University Press, 2006).

3. Ellen G. White, *Fundamentals of Christian Education,* 195.

4. Christine King, *The Nazi State and the New Religions: Five Case Studies in Non-Conformity* (New York: Edwin Mellen Press, 1982), 92.

Nine

"Help! This Is Confusing"

[Attitudes Toward Homosexuality]

This is what they said

- *"Why is it we can embrace drug addicts and alcoholics who are ruining their lives and hurting others, but we can't accept homosexuals who aren't hurting anyone? I'm asking this based on my own experience. Why are some sins more 'acceptable' than others? What would happen if a same-sex couple walked into church? Why can't we accept all people?"*

- *"I'm going to make this short and sweet. I believe I'm a Christian. I'm also a post-op transsexual woman, which means I've had sex reassignment surgery. I've lived as a female since I was thirteen years old, I started hormone therapy at fourteen, then had surgery at nineteen. I live as a woman because that's who I feel I am. I recently discovered the Adventist Church through a co-worker and have been attending for a year now, and no one is the wiser about my situation. But I have questions because I'm considering baptism. I know what the Bible says about homosexuality, but I'm not homosexual. I'm transgender, which means I was born a man, but feel I should have been a woman. I live a very simple life and am concerned about my salvation, which brings me to my question: Is there any hope of me still making it into the kingdom?"*

- *"I work with a group of homosexuals in San Francisco who go from church to church, and the Adventist Church is not on their list of 'friendly' churches to visit. Why are we failing to make homosexuals feel welcome?"*

- *"I feel like a complete failure. I'm active in my church and I completed my undergraduate degree, but no matter what I've accomplished, everything feels overshadowed by one fact—I'm gay. I'll never get married or have children and I'll probably die alone. (Didn't God say that it wasn't good for man to be alone? Oh, that's right. That applies to everyone except people like me.) Please say a prayer for me this week. I don't feel strong enough to endure the road in front of me."*

- *"I'm not homosexual, but when I talk to other people about what the Bible teaches about homosexuality, they don't want to hear it. They call me intolerant and prejudiced. How can I explain my church's point of view without alienating everyone?"*

- *"How can we as a church speak out about homosexuality without coming across as homophobic?"*

- *"Why doesn't the leadership of the church do more to actively discourage homosexuality in our churches? We need to take drastic measures—removing offices from people who condone it or practice it and disfellowshiping people who aren't willing to accept that this is a sin. What is the General Conference doing about this?"*

- *"Is there any reason why homosexuals can't serve as ministers in the Adventist Church?"*

- *"I'm attracted to men. I've been to the Let's Talk Web site before looking for advice, and I have to tell you that it hasn't been very helpful. I've read* Every Young Man's Battle *and that didn't help very much either. My problem is that I can't see my feelings changing, but I also don't see much happiness for me ahead. I know the Bible says we shouldn't have sex with someone of the same gender. What if I fall in love with a man, but don't have sex. Is that OK? I know this sounds absurd. I need to talk to someone who's experienced the homosexual lifestyle and who has broken out of it. I can't bear to listen to advice from someone who has no idea what this feels like."*

- *"When will our church open its eyes and see all the young people who are depressed and alone because their spiritual 'family' won't recognize the reality of what they're going through? Our church is meant to be a place of refuge, but we've certainly made it very clear that there's no room for anyone having problems with homosexuality. I'm frankly disgusted that our church—even at the highest levels—has nothing helpful to say about this."*

- *"I'm interested in finding an Adventist church where I can be open about my sexuality (I'm transgendered). I'm tired of people either ignoring me or making fun of me. I haven't been to church in ten months now. Where can I go? Are there any Adventist churches you know of that will take me in?"*

- *"I'm desperate for my son. He's studying at [an Adventist college] and getting good grades, but he's just overwhelmed with the fact that he's struggling with homosexual feelings. I understand our church's stand on this, but when I'm faced with the reality of the pain he's in, I have to ask, 'Isn't there a better way for us to deal with this issue?' I don't know where to go for help with this, and I'm afraid for what the future holds for our family."*

This is the church speaking to the church. What does it mean and how do we deal with it?

Starting point

My seven-year-old grandson carries within him some of Europe and some of Africa—his mother is from Congo. Perhaps someone at school said something about this to him, but for whatever reason, he said to his mother the other day, "It doesn't matter where you were born; what is important is that you *were* born." When I heard about his comment I thought, *How incredibly insightful—far beyond what he probably understood.*

It doesn't matter how you look, what culture you're from, and how you're "packaged." What matters is that every human being is immeasurably loved and valued by Jesus Christ.

Let this indisputable truth be the backdrop against which we also talk about the question of homosexuality in our society and in our church.

An impasse?

Can anyone fail to sense the intense pain in the voice of the young man who says, "I feel like a complete failure. . . . I don't feel strong enough to endure the road in front of me"? The conundrum we face lies in the tension between clear biblical precepts and the cries for help and calls for acceptance voiced by those whose sexual orientation differs from the biblical model for male and female sexuality. It's a dilemma wrapped up in a tangle of theological perspectives, church standards, and social, political, and cultural attitudes. Further complicating the issue is the fact that in many places around the globe attitudes toward homosexuality are in rapid transition, and we're faced with the reality that what's accepted by some civil authorities may be out of step with biblical norms.

I faced this conundrum in one form or other in almost every one of the live *Let's Talk* broadcasts. But it was the sheer volume of messages I received through the Let's Talk Web site that demonstrated to me how immensely challenging this issue has become for many young Adventist men and women today. Through the relative anonymity of my Web site's "Direct line to the president," I heard from impassioned young people, heartbroken parents, and many, many individuals mired in confusion about their sexual identities, who believed their church had declared them worthless and had abandoned them.

To each one of them, I said, as I did in the *Let's Talk* broadcasts, "The Bible offers no ambiguity as to the rights or wrongs of homosexuality, or that marriage is anything other than the union of a man and woman. The Adventist Church has very specific teachings—firmly grounded in Scripture—about human sexuality. Whether you go to the writings of Paul (Romans 1:24–27; 1 Corinthians 6: 9–11) or to some of the Old Testament narratives, you cannot come away from these without sensing that the homosexual lifestyle is flawed and unacceptable in the eyes of God. There's nothing I read in my Bible that would lead me to any other conclusion."

But I also said—very clearly, I hope—that if the Lord is going to love only perfect people, then I, for one, am in trouble. As a follower of Christ, my first duty is to extend healing to hurting people, and I believe this must determine our approach to any discussion about the question of sexual identities.

It's past time to talk

As I listened to our young people, I heard two strong appeals.

First, I heard them asking their church to acknowledge more clearly the human aspect of this issue. They were asking me to look beyond both pat answers and the limits of my own experience and to see people who are suffering. Some made the point quite forcefully, "How can you presume to understand the experience of those who are struggling with this?" And they were right. I have to accept the limitation that I have not experienced their struggles. But I think it's possible to have compassion for a suffering human being even though I haven't walked exactly the same path. At the very least, it would be a failure not to try.

I heard our young people ask, "When it comes to the issue of homosexuality, why has our church failed to communicate—to both church members and to the wider community—the immeasurable love of our Father for broken human beings?" I heard them say to me, "Please, don't hide behind official church statements; come and meet people who are actually experiencing these struggles. These are people I work with, study with, mix socially with; these are people I care deeply about. And then after I can see that you care about them too, then we can have a conversation about this issue."

A widening chasm

Second, young people told me they're living in a world where attitudes about homosexuality have changed, and are continuing to change—rapidly and dramatically. In many countries of the Western world, these evolving attitudes are remaking our social and legal institutions. As I talked with young men and women, I sensed strongly that many are finding it difficult to reconcile two radically different value systems—the values they absorb from their spiritual family, and the values that surround them as soon as they venture outside the church doors. Every day, many of them are being told that by holding to their biblically grounded understanding of sexuality they're intolerant, prejudiced, and bigoted. Let's not underestimate how significant this problem is for many of our young people who aren't gay or lesbian themselves.

"Please," some of them are saying to their church, "help me work through this. Help me develop the tools I need to translate my spiritual values into the everyday reality of the world in which I live."

I heard others say, "Why do we keep focusing on this issue? Society is done with it—why aren't we?" But this is precisely another source of tension for our church. While some of our younger members are calling on their spiritual family to "get over it; just move on and accept homosexuality as part of reality and focus on other aspects of life," others are saying, "We have to talk about this. The media headlines are dominated by gay-rights issues or the same-sex marriage debate, but our churches remain 'discussion-free zones' when it comes to homosexuality."

Clearly, we don't have the option—if we ever did—of simply looking the other way.

Limits to Christian love?

Are we willing to dialogue with our young people about this? Make no mistake: homosexuality is an extraordinarily difficult issue for us to talk about, and one I believe that will continue to grow even more difficult in the years ahead. Why? In part, because a genuine dialogue becomes difficult when I come to the table with parameters or norms that are nonnegotiable. For me, the question comes down to this: Can I truly love and am I willing to engage with an individual whose lifestyle—chosen or otherwise, chemical mismatch or preference—I consider fundamentally wrong? Am I able to listen with some degree of credible understanding to his or her pains, fears, and confusion, without communicating—either by spoken word or body language—any hint of condemnation or rejection?

There's no doubt in my mind that Christ would reach out to these men and women with compassion and care, and that today He's asking no less of me and the church. How are we doing on this? I confess I find this difficult, and I don't think I've done very well.

A strong element of what I heard from our young people was simply disappointment and perhaps disillusionment. They asked, "Why does the church I love come across as unloving? Why are we letting ourselves be painted as a judgmental and harsh community? Is that what we are?"

I was interested to read the results of a study published just a few years ago that suggests more than 90 percent of young non-Christians in the United States—and some 80 percent of Christian young people—believe that Christians show "excessive contempt and unloving attitudes towards gays and lesbians."[1] One of the most frequent criticisms leveled by these young people was that the church had made homosexuality a bigger sin than anything else.

Is it possible that most of us can live somewhat complacently with "smaller" sins that we accommodate as part of normal life, while other sins gather a stigma of contempt and disgust that makes them particularly repulsive? Is this the message we're implicitly sending to our young people?

Many of the Christian young people questioned in this study also said their church hasn't helped them understand and apply biblical teaching on homosexuality to their friendships with gays and lesbians. They suggest, quite correctly, that the biblical narrative about homosexuality uses language that's fundamentally different from that used in today's discussions about gays and lesbians.

What's the result? When our young people talk about homosexuality with someone who rejects the biblical perspective, they're faced with a vast, seemingly impassable gulf of linguistic, moral, social, and theological difference. Is it any wonder that even hearing each other, let alone understanding each other, is so incredibly difficult?

And so again we come back to the heart of our challenge: which has the greater importance—being right or being kind?

With Christ, it must be possible to carry both of these values into our conversations and our relationships.

Opening up the church doors — to people

There's a YouTube clip of a recently produced film in which a homosexual woman seeks to explain why she's not welcome at her local Adventist church. "Church members want to keep their church pure," she says. "They want to keep it pure."

It's an uncomfortable accusation. Is it true? Is a vain attempt to keep our churches "pure" a factor at play here? Do we see excluding certain people—for whatever reasons—as a means of maintaining the integrity of our values and beliefs? And if so, where did we get that idea? How do we reconcile this with the mission assignment given to us by Christ?

The church exists in an environment that's anything but pure, and our mission is to a very sinful world. Should we be surprised that the church is filled with sinners? If we try to seek purity through excluding "impure" people, then we'll find our pews not just sparsely occupied but empty. We just have to know who we are and why, and then get on with the task of communicating Christ the Savior and treating people as He would.

Upholding biblical truth doesn't require that we forgo compassion. Offering love and acceptance to individuals—no matter what issues they're struggling with—doesn't compromise our commitment to the truths of Scripture. It's not an either-or situation. It's a "because" situation. *Because* we're followers of Christ, He requires us to extend to everyone His unqualified love for humanity, even as we hold true to our biblical convictions about human sexuality.

Should we change our tone of voice?

How can we respond to the pleas of our young people for a more engaged approach when it comes relating to homosexuality personally, as well as communicating our church's position to the broader community?

For a start, I'd suggest that merely reiterating our biblically grounded standards is not enough. This, alone, doesn't help our young people navigate the complexities they face. They know what the Bible says. For them, the spirit and attitude with which we communicate our convictions is of critical importance.

What they need is a dialectic that allows them to engage with the voices that label all religious people as prejudiced, or that tells them that their church rejects homosexuals. Young people need to know how to demolish the false dichotomy that says they must choose between faithfulness and compassion, that tells them that by reaching out to those struggling with sexual identity they're somehow compromising their commitment to biblical values.

Would it help to remind our young people, and ourselves, that while the Adventist Church holds strongly to biblical models of sexuality, we're also strong on upholding human dignity, and we place a premium on developing respectful dialogues with others—no matter how far we may differ on certain issues?

Let's tell our communities that we'll always oppose hate-filled rhetoric that serves to inflame violence and that reinforces the gulf that divides us; that we'll always speak up whenever a group in society is singled out for scorn and derision, let alone abuse, because of their race, ethnicity, or sexual orientation. Let's not just tell but show our communities that we believe every human being is created in the image of God and is dearly loved by Him.

[Conversation starters]

Do you want to explore more deeply some of the issues raised in this chapter? Here are some ideas for starting a dialogue between younger and older members of your congregation.

1. **Have your say**. Apart from Scripture, are there any other factors that may have influenced your opinion about how Adventist Christians should relate to homosexuality?

2. **Conversation builders.**
   - In a survey of young Americans, 91 percent of non-Christians chose the term *anti-homosexual* as best describing the Christian faith. (Eighty percent of church-going young people chose the same word!)[2] How could this be? What's driving these perceptions?

   - Imagine your local newspaper asks for your comment on same-sex marriage or another gay-rights issue. How would you explain the church's stance on homosexuality while also communicating Christ's unequivocal love for every person?

   - Christian writer Rachel Held Evans suggests that if Christians choose to fight a culture war against gay rights, they'll lose a generation of young believers.[3] Is she right, or is the reality less clear cut?

3. **Discussion questions.**
   - The old adage "hate the sin, love the sinner" has sometimes been used by Christians in relation to homosexuality. Is this helpful? What does "loving the sinner" require?

   - Do you think gays would find your church a welcoming environment?

   - If a young person in your church was struggling with issues of sexual identity, would your congregation be a safe place for him or her to find guidance?

   - Do Adventist Christians have a duty to speak up about gay rights issues currently on the public agenda?

What now? During His ministry on earth, Jesus spoke plainly about right and wrong, and yet He was called a "friend to sinners" (Matthew 11:19).

- Why do you think sinners were comfortable in His presence?

- In welcoming homosexuals into your congregation, what changes in attitudes or practices would help your church better reflect Christ's example?

[Endnotes]

1. David Kinnaman and Gabe Lyons, *UnChristian: What a New Generation Really Thinks About Christianity . . . and Why It Matters* (Grand Rapids, Mich.: Baker Books, 2007), 92, 93.

2. Kinnaman and Lyons, *UnChristian,* 92, 93.

3. Rachel Held Evans, "How to Win a Culture War and Lose a Generation," *Rachel Held Evans* (blog), accessed November 28, 2012, http://rachelheldevans.com/blog/win-culture-war-lose-generation-amendment-one-north-carolina.

Ten

"It's Different Now"

This is what they said

- *"Why will the Adventist Church remove from membership someone for 'living in sexual immorality' but not for a myriad [of] other sins that Jesus Himself seemed to place great emphasis on—like pride, arrogance, self-righteousness, divisiveness, and being judgmental? It seems to me that these sins are a whole lot more harmful to the church than two people who love each other and who've chosen their own way of making their commitment before God."*

- *"At the church where I was a member for four years, I witnessed a women being disciplined for divorcing her abusive husband. Why should she have been disciplined? Did the church really want her to stay in such a horrible relationship? . . . After everything I saw, I don't think I want to get married. Why should I take the chance of ending up in the same position?"*

- *"My friends and I find it funny that when an unmarried couple discovers the lady is pregnant, they quickly get married in order to avoid getting disfellowshiped. Basically, that's their only choice if they want to stay in the church. It really makes the whole concept of marriage pretty ridiculous."*

- *"I have a friend who lives with a boy in [a European country] and they still live together. Both are baptized Adventists and they have one child, with another one on the way. They are thinking they might finally have enough money to get married, but they want to know if they can get married in an Adventist Church. What is the Adventist doctrine on this?"*

- *"I am engaged to a woman who goes to the same church as me, and I did a wrong thing. She's pregnant. I have confessed to God and I believe He has forgiven me. But when I went to the church elders to talk about it, they say the Adventist pastor can't perform the marriage. Pastor Paulsen, what is the church's position on this? Am I that unholy that I can't marry in the church?"*

- *"What is the church's stance on cohabitation? I'm not talking about casual relationships—but I'm talking about a committed relationship that, in eyes of practically everyone, is the same as being married. Is the marriage ceremony itself necessary if you've already made your vows to God privately?"*

- *"Why should a wedding and a document from the state be the only way of sanctifying a marriage? As far as I can tell, the Bible doesn't give a precise formula."*

- *"My question is about my standing in the Adventist Church. I moved in with a nonbelieving woman four years ago, but I've been coming back to church lately. She doesn't want to get married, and I don't want to leave her just because she won't go through a wedding. No one seems willing to help me understand the consequences of my situation. Obviously, I can't take part in any official ministry of the church (can I?). I don't know where I belong at all. Someone suggested that I should get rebaptized. Is that necessary?"*

- *"I'm living with my partner currently—we're not baptized because we're 'living in sin,' and they won't baptize us until we are married. To some people who aren't in the church and haven't grown up in the church, this is a block. For example, my fiancée's parents have been living together for thirty years. They are not married, and they are not going to get married. If someone says to them, 'You can't get baptized unless you get married,' they are going to reply, 'Well, you can keep your religion.'"*

- *"This may be a strange question to you—it's about my grandfather who is a widower. He recently moved in with a lady who also lost her husband some time ago. They are both Adventist Church members. I think everyone at their church thinks they've been married by a judge—but they haven't because she doesn't want to lose her Social Security benefits. Does the Adventist Church recognize this type of 'marriage'? They are 100 percent committed to each other and to the church. I can't really see any moral problem with two people living together in a committed relationship without going through a marriage ceremony."*

- *"In our culture, paying* lobola *(the bride price paid to the family of the bride-to-be) is recognized as marrying—even before the white wedding. My question is, is it OK to sleep with your partner after paying* lobola? *And if so, what's the point of the wedding?"*

- *"My concern is with the unreality of the abstinence ideal. In the real world, this just isn't happening. Marriage and sex before marriage are areas where there seems to a disconnect between standards that we're told are absolute, and the reality of the world in which young people live. Most of my friends are in committed relationships. Are we all doomed?"*

- *"I do understand the reasoning behind abstinence, and I know that marriage is a holy institution. Maybe it's just me (although I don't think so), but does anyone actually 'save themselves for marriage' anymore?"*

This is the church speaking to the church. What does it mean and how do we deal with it?

This matters . . . now

It's probably not surprising that throughout the seven years of the Let's Talk initiative, a significant proportion of all the questions and comments I received from Seventh-day Adventist young people related to their church's stance on sexual relationships, marriage, and cohabitation. It's at this age—from the late teens through to the early thirties—that young people are grappling with powerful, competing messages about how and when they should form intimate relationships. They must somehow reconcile the clear moral stance of their church family with the pervasive, seemingly attractive, countermessages from various media. They observe the example of their peers, and they feel the conflicting pull of their convictions and their desires. Spiritual, social, cultural, and physical forces are at work, and so it's little wonder that there's ample scope for confusion and mistakes.

And yet it would be glib to simply leave the issue here, for through the voices of our young people I hear signals of more serious trends within society—especially within Western cultures—that challenge the way our church teaches the younger generation about the biblical model for marriage and family.

The new "normal"

In Europe, the rate of cohabitation is such that it has largely shed its bygone flavor of dubious morality in the eyes of the general public. In Sweden, for instance, well over half of all babies born are to couples who aren't married, and many European countries have developed legal protections for those who enter domestic partnerships.[1] In the United States, cohabitation rates have increased more than seventeenfold over the past fifty years, with the greatest jump occurring in the past decade.[2] Today, statistics show that in North America a majority of young adults will, at one point or another, live in a domestic partnership, and more than half of all marriages will be preceded by cohabitation.[3]

What do these statistics mean? To put it simply, cohabitation before marriage, or as an alternative to marriage, is becoming the new normal in popular thinking. And this is the message being delivered to the public, loudly and clearly, through television, literature, music, and all manner of other pop culture media, and thereby also to Seventh-day Adventist young people.

Our own Valuegenesis studies bear out the influence of changing cultural norms on the thinking and decision making of Adventist young people in some parts of the world. Although the data was collected almost a decade ago, some 20 percent of Adventist high school students in North America who participated in the Valuegenesis2 study said it was morally OK for two adults who loved each other to have a sexual relationship. An additional 15 percent weren't sure.[4]

Young Adventist writer Nathan Brown is probably reflecting the views of many in his generation when he observes, "These trends pose some tough questions in relation to our church's stand on marriage, particularly in relation to 'discipline' procedures and the impact these have on the involvement on young people in our church." He goes on to ask, Is the Adventist Church "more interested in a wedding or in commitment?"[5]

Of course, marriage and commitment are not in tension. If a man and a woman have chosen to walk together into the future and are prepared to make that fundamental commitment to each other and to God, why not express that commitment to the public in a way that's universally understood by the public, namely through a wedding?

But for some of our young people, the question remains, is a wedding *necessary* for commitment? How should we respond?

Embracing all people, not all values

When it comes to marriage and sexual relationships, popular culture often paints religious institutions either as quaint and wildly out-of-touch, or as harsh, strident champions of a bygone morality.

How do we sound to our young people when we talk to them about God's ideal for human relationships? What principles should guide our message and tone of voice?

I believe our starting point is simply this: The church, as God's chosen instrument to communicate the gospel of salvation in Christ Jesus, will reach out to embrace all people. There is no one who shall not be wanted and loved by the church. Yet, at the same time, the church can't be a body of maximum accommodation for all points of view, constantly shifting and adjusting her values and personality to fit the broadest possible spectrum of human opinion.

The church represents and carries a defined set of values, and we derive these from the Bible. When we voluntarily join the family of faith, we choose to carry the same values. This isn't only because these values describe the community we've joined, but because these values have now become part of our *own* identities. In that process, we leave behind some things that are in tension with biblical values. We leave the worldly behind, and the life of the Spirit and the fruit this brings, take over. Maybe it's not a very fast or even a very successful transformation, but our paths have changed, and we're headed in a new direction.

Failure happens. What then?

When we communicate biblically based sexual standards to our young people, do we also talk to them about the reality of sin, forgiveness, and redemption? The biblical rights and wrongs may seem so high and beyond reach. Each of us in our everyday lives bears testimony to the reality of the struggle between good and evil. We can say, with the apostle Paul, "I have the desire to do what is good, but I cannot carry it out. For I do not do the good I want to do, but the evil I do not want to do—this I keep on doing" (Romans 7:18, 19, NIV).

However, regardless how often we fail, it doesn't do away with the values and standards of a Spirit-led life. It simply means we haven't lived up to our potential. We may have disappointed many people, probably none more so than ourselves, but our shortcomings don't justify a revision of God-given standards and values.

As Christians, failure can leave us alternately gazing into the distance at the seemingly unreachable beauty of the life God offers us, and staring full in the face of our own frailty. The distance between the two may seem too great for us—and may in fact *be* great. We become depressed and discouraged, and we may say to ourselves, "I'm not going to make it! It's hopeless!"

Well, not so quick. When we talk to our young people about the standards God calls them to in their sexual relationships, let's not leave the story there.

Christ saves failures

We're just sinners, all of us, and we each experience in our own bodies the tension of the war between good and evil. But God is in the business of saving sinners—and He's good at it. Therefore, whatever our failings may be, we remain within the reach of God's salvation unless we make a deliberate choice to walk away from Him. He who said, "I am the way. . . . No one comes to the Father except through me" (John 14:6, NIV) cares profoundly for failing human beings; and none of us, however good or bad, is a finished product.

The important point to keep in mind here is that failure doesn't equal being lost! So, let's encourage each other and give each other hope. Let's not be quick in passing judgment—especially on our young. I've noticed that people don't generally do very well when they're the object—or victim—of another person's spiritual assessment and judgment.

The question inevitably then comes: How should we, as a church, deal with those who make mistakes in their marriage and relationships? How do we keep them from simply walking away, yet still affirm the standards that Scripture gives us for sexual relationships? The incredible wonder of Christ's example is that He never failed to love sinners and draw them close, yet didn't lower the standard for how His children should live.

Putting theory into practice

As a church, most of our difficulties don't lie on the side of uncertainty about biblical teachings on this issue. We're able to lay out a clear, neat theological framework. But real-life situations? They can get messy.

Consider some of the questions and comments from Adventist young people that introduced this chapter.

Is sex outside marriage a greater sin than other more garden-variety sins, such as pride, arrogance, and self-righteousness?

I know of no way to make a safe and reliable sliding scale of sin's "greatness," or otherwise. The Bible doesn't give me the criteria to do that. In grading sin the first problem we're up against is our common tendency to think of sin in terms of a series of specific acts or actions. We did something or we said something, and we believe this identifies and describes our sin. But at most, this is probably just one phase of the sin problem.

The Bible leads us to understand sin in the context of the whole life we choose to live. Is the Lord no longer my most important Friend and Partner in life? Do my values and choices effectively make God redundant in my life? Have I found other "gods" more appealing? Our answers to these questions will inevitably become public, for our behavior and choices are an outward expression of who we really are. If we choose selfishness, our behavior reflects our choice and we will become destructive, hurtful, and harmful. That's how sin expresses itself.

Are some actions worse than others? Probably. Why? I think the answer lies, in part, in the extent of the damage that some sin can inflict.

Sexual sin brings hurt and destruction not just to ourselves but to many other people as well. Often, the consequences of our actions are on public display, and thus have an even greater reach and impact. The circle of devastation can be wide—far wider than we could have imagined. Don't underestimate the gravity of hurting another person. It's impossible to read Christ's words in Matthew 25 without realizing how profoundly He cares how we treat each other.

Of course, pride, arrogance, and self-righteousness can be more inwardly contained—but eventually these will find ways of expressing themselves outwardly, causing damage and destruction to others. Pride and self-righteousness close the heart to the workings of the Spirit. In Christ's encounters with the Pharisees, it was their "pride and prejudice" that closed their hearts to His message.[6] Let no one underestimate the seriousness of such sins, although their presence may take on a more subtle life in each of us.

It's not for us to guess the mind of God who sees the heart and knows our motives. He's the only one who can safely judge us; but He will call us to account. Let's just be clear about what the Bible teaches is right and wrong and do our best to order our lives accordingly, while we live kindly and lovingly together.

What about divorce, remarriage, and church discipline?

How do the standards of the church meet the everyday realities of marriages that break up, and where one, or both, partners seek a new life with someone else? Is church discipline an effective instrument for dealing with situations that involve so much heartbreak and impact so many people?

The church has consistently taken the view that marriage is a life-long commitment between a man and a woman, and it's also a covenant between a couple and God. But no one should be surprised that marriages will often hit difficult spots. After all, two different people—sometimes *very* different—are learning to live together in a harmonious and loving relationship. Sometimes it doesn't work. For one reason or another, marriages fail, and divorce—with all its confusion and hurt—is the result. When this happens, our loving heavenly Father reaches out and offers healing. How can the church do any less?

In this instance, I believe the church has a dual responsibility: it must make all efforts to offer healing, and it must also protect and affirm biblical standards for moral conduct. If you're going to discipline someone, then make sure you've also made every conceivable effort to demonstrate that you care deeply and profoundly for that person.

The historic position of our church has been that if one spouse is unfaithful, and the relationship can't be healed, this is a biblical ground for divorce and remarriage.[7] When the world church met for its General Conference Session in 2000 in Toronto, Canada, it restated this understanding of the biblical standard for divorce and remarriage. But new language was also introduced into the *Church*

Manual describing more fully what we understand by "unfaithfulness to the marriage vow." It says, "The New Testament word for fornication includes certain other sexual irregularities (1 Cor. 6: 9; 1 Tim. 1: 9, 10; Rom. 1: 24–27)." It then specifically lists incest, child sexual abuse, and homosexual practices as "just cause for separation or divorce"—each of these is "unfaithfulness to the marriage vow," and gives the right to remarry.[8]

The church has also had an equally clear position regarding church discipline in the divorce and remarriage scenario. The spouse who has violated the marriage vow and been divorced and who then remarries is placed, by the local church, under church discipline. Normally, this means they're removed from membership for a specified period of time.

For me, the critical point in this exercise is that the local church, both as a body and as individuals, understands that placing someone under church discipline is *not an exercise in shunning*. If we don't make a deliberate and concerted effort to love and heal erring members—to keep them from walking out the door—we've failed both those individuals and our Lord.

Cohabitation: What's the church's stance on this?

It's striking the extent to which Western pop culture portrays cohabitation—unmarried couples living together, socially and sexually—as utterly normal. In making that observation I've immediately revealed that I belong to a somewhat more "mature" generation, for I suspect that the idea of cohabitation holds little shock value for most of our younger church members. Why? Quite simply, because it's a fixture in the social landscape into which they were born.

Some couples choose cohabitation for a while, as a kind of trial run, while they get to know each other better. Many are in a cohabitation relationship that signifies their serious commitment to each other. As marriage is a commitment for life, they see cohabitation as a similar bond. They don't plan for anything other than to continue to live together, build a home, and have children. In some countries, this arrangement can be publicly registered and given fiscal security, including the right to inherit, on a basis similar to marriage. In such countries, cohabitation is viewed by the public, in general, as an acceptable alternative to traditional marriage.

Should the church also see it this way?

No. Cohabitation, notwithstanding the serious commitment of some couples, is not understood internationally and cross-culturally as a union similar to marriage. It's vulnerable to more uncertainties: in the same way it can be easily entered into, so it can also be dissolved with relative legal ease. It's not the most stable environment in which to have children and build a family.

The question I'd put to a couple planning to live together is, "Why not just get married? It's a union and a status everyone understands. If your commitment is really as serious as you claim—and I don't question that—why not do it the established and honorable way? Is there a problem with that?"

I suspect that some, if they honestly examine their motives, will admit that the built-in escape clause offered by cohabitation is attractive to them. The thought is, "If this doesn't work out, ending it will be less complicated."

What about a man and women who've lived together in cohabitation and who want to set their lives in order before God, the church, the public, their families, and themselves? Could their marriage ceremony be performed in an Adventist church? I don't see why not. It's like any other conversion step. People who've lived one kind of life but who now want to align themselves with biblical values are enthusiastically embraced by the church. Why should this case be any different?

Change the narrative?

We can't simply wish away the fact that much of society today sees cohabitation as an acceptable—perhaps preferable—alternative to marriage and views sexual abstinence before marriage as abnormal. Marriage has a serious image problem, and this is our reality. This is the world we're called to love and to reach with Christ's salvation, and in which our young people are growing, learning, and forming relationships.

Perhaps we need to do a better job at broadening the message we deliver to our young people about marriage and relationships. Yes, we need to speak plainly about the dos and don'ts of sexual morality. But could it be that we've neglected to clearly communicate to them the incredible rewards that marriage can bring? Do we tell them about the matchless joy they'll find in building the kind of vibrant, loving partnership God intends for them? Do they *see* the truth of this in our marriage relationships?

Marriage between a man and a woman is God ordained. Only this kind of union, in which two become "one flesh," meets the biblical standard of marriage. It's a union in which the joy of a sexual life creates and serves the bonding between a man and a woman. And when we follow God's guidelines, marriage can become an unparalleled physical, emotional, and spiritual relationship.

[Conversation starters]

Do you want to explore more deeply some of the issues raised in this chapter? Here are some ideas for starting a dialogue between younger and older members of your congregation.

1. **Have your say.** As young people (or former young people), what are the most important messages you need to hear from parents, teachers, or local church leaders about marriage and cohabitation?

2. **Conversation builders.**
   - From television's *Modern Family* to *Married With Children,* popular culture has a lot to say about the institution of marriage. What are some of the negative stereotypes people absorb from what they watch or read?

   - In a recent *New York Times* article, the author talks about the so-called cohabitation effect. She writes: "Couples who cohabit before marriage (and especially before an engagement or an otherwise clear commitment) tend to be less satisfied with their marriages—and more likely to divorce—than couples who do not."[9] Why do you think this could be so?

   - Lawmakers in Mexico City recently suggested the idea of "renewable marriage licenses" where a couple can specify a length of time (two years or more) after which they'll need to renew their commitment.[10] Do you think a fear of commitment ("until death do us part") is driving the trend toward choosing cohabitation over marriage?

3. **Discussion questions.**
   - What makes a marriage, a marriage? A legal document? A wedding ceremony? Sexual intimacy? A clear commitment, private or otherwise, made between two people?

   - How far do you think our attitudes toward marriage are shaped by the examples of married life—happy or otherwise—we see in our family or church?

   - Do we assume that if we've told young people what the Bible says about marriage and relationships, we've successfully communicated all they need to know? Is there more we should be saying or doing?

- Is the climate of your congregation one that would encourage young people to seek guidance and support if they're struggling with relationship issues?

What now? What specific resources or programs could your congregation provide young people to help them "decide, rather than slide" when it comes to forming intimate relationships?

[Endnotes]

1. European Commission Eurostat, "Live Births Outside Marriage 2011," accessed December 4, 2012, http://epp.eurostat.ec.europa.eu/tgm/table.do?tab=table&init=1&language=en&pcode=tps00018&plugin=0.

2. W. Bradford Wilcox, ed., *The State of Our Unions: Marriage in America 2011* (Charlottesville, Va.: National Marriage Project at the University of Virginia and the Center for Marriage and Families at the Institute for American Values, 2010), 75.

3. Paul R. Amato, Alan Booth, David R. Johnson, and Stacy J. Rogers, *Alone Together: How Marriage in America Is Changing* (Cambridge, Mass.: Harvard University Press, 2007), 21.

4. "It's All About Values," *Update* 9 (March 2003): 2. This newsletter about the Valuegenesis2 study was published by La Sierra University's John Hancock Center for Youth and Family Ministry and the North American Division Office of Education.

5. Nathan Brown, "Ceremony or Commitment," *Spectrum Magazine* (blog), February 28, 2007, accessed December 4, 2012, http://spectrummagazine.org/blog/2007/02/28/ceremony-or-commitment.

6. Ellen G. White, *Selected Messages,* 1:70.

7. For a fuller discussion, see "Chapter 7: Discipline," *Seventh-day Adventist Church Manual,* 18th ed. (Silver Spring, Md.: General Conference of Seventh-day Adventists Secretariat, 2010), 56–67.

8. Ibid., 62.

9. Meg Jay, "The Downside of Cohabiting Before Marriage," Sunday Review, *New York Times,* April 14, 2012, accessed December 4, 2012, http://www.nytimes.com/2012/04/15/opinion/sunday/the-downside-of-cohabiting-before-marriage.html?pagewanted=all&_r=0.

10. Christina Ng, "Mexico City Considers Temporary Marriage Licenses," *ABC News* (blog), September 30, 2011, accessed December 4, 2012, http://abcnews.go.com/blogs/headlines/2011/09/mexico-city-considers-temporary-marriage-licenses/.

Eleven

"Is She Still Relevant?"

[Understanding Ellen White]

This is what they said

- *"Could you please look at this Web site link I came across recently? I think you should look at it. It's about why Adventism is 'evil' and how Mrs. White was a 'fraud.' It really offended me as an Adventist, but I am starting to wonder about a lot of things. Some of what they say seems reasonable. Anyway, please just look at the site. It has opened my eyes to what some people think of the Adventist Church."*

- *"In one of Ellen White's books (I'm not sure which one) she wrote that chess should not to be played. Why shouldn't chess be played? Does it have to do with something bad that the game represented back then, or is there something wrong with chess itself? I started playing chess a couple of years ago, and these comments from Ellen White have just been brought to my attention. Mrs. White also said that we are not to go to bowling alleys. In my country of Jamaica there are few, if any, bowling alleys, hence I am ignorant as to what else could take place at a bowling alley (apart from bowling). So please enlighten me as to why it's wrong to visit a bowling alley."*

- *"I read in* Messages to Young People *by Ellen G. White that fiction is a pretty terrible thing and that the 'mind is ruined which is allowed to be adsorbed in story-reading.' But are all fiction books wrong and bad? And if some fiction is OK, then what are we meant to do with Mrs. White's comments about this?"*

- *"Can someone be baptized into the Seventh-day Adventist Church without believing that the gift of prophecy was manifested in the ministry of Ellen G. White. I'd like to know. Thanks."*

- *"I am bothered about our fellow Adventist members who are leaving the church because of our doctrine on the infallibility of Ellen White's writings. I'm not a theology graduate, but I really want to know our position on this because it hurts me when somebody calls our church a cult."*

- *"I am a junior in high school. I was born and raised in [another denomination] but was brought into the Seventh-day Adventist Church, and it changed my life. Some Adventists I talk with say that Ellen G. White is not actually a prophetess, but others talk about her as if she's an equal to the authors of the Bible. Please explain to me why Ellen G. White was different from any other person or church founder. Please explain to me who this woman is!"*

- *"I think that everyone who's been raised an Adventist can understand why most of us [young people] just tune out when people start quoting Ellen White at us. It's like her writings are used as ammunition to keep us in line. Personally, I feel like I should pay more attention to what she says, and I probably need to read her for myself. I can't get past all the negativity, though."*

- *"I'm in a relationship with a man who doesn't share my Adventist beliefs. Now he is researching about Ellen G. White and he says she's not a prophet and that some of the things she writes are contradictory. So my question is: What can I do to help him? I don't know all the answers, and I don't know where to find them. I've never really thought about it before."*

- *"Is Ellen G. White really a prophet despite some false prophecies some people believe she made (such as the Shut Door Doctrine)? Thanks."*

- *"I love my church and I believe what it teaches. But I think, at some level, I just prefer to not think too much about the meaning of Ellen White to our church. Why? Because I can't relate to what I read in her books. I appreciate the fact that she was a strong and incredible woman who we, as Adventists, owe so much to. But if someone was to ask me, point blank, whether I thought she was a prophet (like the prophets of the Bible), I'm not sure what I would say."*

- *"Some people say that you can find an Ellen White quote for just about any position you want to prove. I think that we do that a lot. For me, I think we rely too much on her. Why can't we get everything we need from the Bible?"*

- *"Do you think that Mrs. White is still relevant to the church today? What she wrote about was so focused on what was happening in her day, I don't think we can just apply it today, can we?"*

- *"I don't really have an opinion about Ellen White. Do I have to? How important is it to being an Adventist?"*

- *"The Spirit of Prophecy is a gift to the Adventist Church, so why don't we value it more? Why doesn't the leadership of the church do more to help young people understand how precious this gift is? In a lot of churches I've attended, it seems like we're embarrassed to talk and preach about her."*

Well, there we are. This is what some of our young people are thinking and saying. How should we respond to their comments?

Tell me who she is

Perhaps the most significant chunk of correspondence I received about the ministry of Ellen White relates in some way to her role and authority in our church.

As I reread the messages these young people sent, I remember an incident in my own life. As a young doctoral student at Tubingen University in Germany, I found myself in a seminar seated around a long table with the professor and about twenty other students. The professor, who knew I was a Seventh-day Adventist, suddenly turned to me and asked, with no prior warning, "You Adventists have a woman in your history who you consider a prophet. Tell us, Jan, what was her role and what is her authority in your church today?"

Most present, including my professor, were conservative Lutherans who knew little about Adventism or its beliefs. Further, there was the tendency in that particular university community, and also more widely in Europe, to label Adventism as a sect, and exhibit A in support of this idea was the role of Ellen White within our church.

The other students waited to see how I would respond.

I've never felt embarrassed or apologetic about the role of Ellen White in our church, and so I told the group, "Yes, we consider her a prophet."

I said: "The prophetic gift is one of many gifts of the Spirit that we should properly expect to find in the church—this is very much in harmony with what Paul presents to the believers in Corinth. It's a biblical reality; it should be expected, and shouldn't by itself be seen as a cultic phenomenon, or something that requires justification."

No one around the table objected, and so I went on.

I told them I didn't believe the prophetic ministry had simply disappeared for the almost two thousand years since Christianity began.

"Isn't it possible that the Reformer Martin Luther was himself endowed with the prophetic gift as he led the church into the Reformation of the sixteenth century?" I asked these staunch Lutherans. "He clearly was an extraordinary servant of God—but his writings weren't infallible and they weren't an addition to the Bible, and they certainly weren't meant to suggest doctrines not otherwise found in Scripture."

Adventists hold that this is true for the writings of Ellen White, I explained. She called her writings a lesser light to lead people to the greater light, the Bible, and that's how we view her writings today. Her counsels aren't an addition to the biblical canon, and they aren't meant to perform the function of the Bible.

I pointed out that a prophet doesn't necessarily get everything right. Prophetic ministry is an evolving ministry, nurtured by the presence of the Holy Spirit. It's a ministry that addresses specific needs that, presumably, are what precipitated the prophetic gift at that particular time.

"Who are we to read the mind of God?" I asked the group. "Do we dare claim to know precisely all the 'whys' as to the timing and circumstances of various gifts of the Spirit? Who are we to make a reliable list of what we judge as genuine occurrences of these gifts throughout the history of the church?"

In answer to the question about Ellen White's authority for our church, I said, "Yes, she has authority as she addresses various issues and challenges that we meet on our journey, as she underscores and promotes the mission of the church, and as she speaks to our spiritual growth."

Searching for a better way to explain what I was trying to say, I added, "It's just like most traditional Lutherans wouldn't want to stray very far from the Augsburg Confession" (the twenty-eight articles of belief, dating from the sixteenth century, which make up the basic confession of the Lutheran faith).

And that ended the discussion.

Regardless of whether or not I succeeded in dispelling some misconceptions, the memory of that incident has stayed with me. I learned that people who aren't familiar with our faith—along with some who ought to know better—can find the ministry of Ellen White an obstacle to their understanding of Adventism. And I found that the best response is to speak clearly and without apology, placing the prophetic gift of Mrs. White squarely within its rightful context of biblical legitimacy.

Feeding false perceptions?

Let's never forget that we—individuals Adventists—bear a large part in shaping how others view the role of Ellen White's ministry in our church. It's *our* responsibility to make sure we don't use her writings in ways that foster misunderstandings or feed into cultic misconceptions.

We must be clear: The writings of Ellen White are not an addition to the Bible. The biblical canon is closed, and her writings are not part of it. Adventist doctrines and our spiritual and moral values rest on Scripture. We must show discernment in the way we use the precious gift of her writings, not only to avoid misunderstandings within the wider community but also in the minds of own people—particularly the young.

Messages from our pulpits must be built on the Bible. Pastors and church leaders, read the Bible to your congregation and leave no doubt that this is the source of your message. This is precisely what Ellen White counseled us to do, and she wouldn't have wanted it otherwise. Her writings have an important part to play in magnifying and amplifying the biblical message, but what is a preacher implying if his or her Sabbath morning sermon is built largely around a string of Ellen White quotes?

First impressions

One of the key challenges when it comes to introducing Ellen White's ministry to our young people is starting off on the right foot.

I remember my own experience as an Adventist teenager. Like so many teens, I suffered from low self-esteem. I felt picked on—by members in my church, by the preacher from the pulpit, and by God. There were more teenage mistakes in my life than I care to remember, and I sometimes despaired that I would ever measure up. I was convinced that, should I appear before God's judgment seat there and then, I wouldn't have a ghost of a chance. For a young boy who really wanted to be a good Seventh-day Adventist, it was discouraging, to say the least.

And then into this mix came Ellen White's book *Messages to Young People.* Reading it, as I did in my early teens, reinforced my low self-esteem and brought me to the brink of spiritual hopelessness.

Some years afterward, in my late teens, I read her book *Steps to Christ,* followed by *Thoughts From the Mount of Blessing.* And that was my survival. In reading and rereading *Steps to Christ,* I met my Savior. My sense of unworthiness didn't disappear, but I knew my salvation was secure. With my faith firmly anchored in the loving embrace of my Savior, I reread *Messages to Young People* and this time, my experience was radically different.

From the perspective of later years, it's easy to forget how vulnerable the young mind and heart can be. Nurturing a young person's love and respect for the ministry of Ellen White means being thoughtful in the way we share her writings; it means providing context about her role and authority within our church; and, it means creating an environment where young people feel safe to air their questions.

Defining "authority"

When it comes to Ellen White's authority, perhaps the most frequent question I received from the young was, "OK, you make the distinction between her writings and the Bible. Are you saying that her inspiration and authority are on a different level?"

My answer is that prophetic authority is defined by *function*. If we try to use Mrs. White's writings to perform a function for which they were neither given nor intended, their authority is compromised. Our spiritual beliefs, every doctrine we accept, must all rest on the Bible. That's what *sola scriptura* means. If we can't base a particular doctrinal position on Scripture, then we must let it go!

The prophetic ministry of Ellen White was given to encourage us on our spiritual journey, to help us understand the values we must treasure, and to guide us in discharging our God-given mission as we prepare for the return of our Lord. As she provides this guidance, she is an inspired messenger of the Lord. This is her function, and in this she has clear authority as a spokesperson for God.

Are her writings infallible? She herself says, "No."

She wrote: "God and heaven alone are infallible."[1] And again: "In regard to infallibility, I never claimed it; God alone is infallible. His word is true, and in Him is no variableness or shadow of turning."[2]

Even so, do we still sometimes use her words as though they were infallible? If we do, we're disregarding her own warning and the clear word of Scripture. We must be able to understand the scope of her God-given function, *without* undermining the spiritual authority of her counsel.

Real-world application

It became very clear through the *Let's Talk* broadcasts and Web site that many young people encounter challenges in applying the words of Ellen White to the daily realities of their twenty-first-century lives. This is especially true when it comes to their recreational choices. They ask, "Mrs. White has written so much about entertainment, games, sport, and pleasure-seeking activities. Some of her counsel I can understand, but some I can't. For example, what's wrong with playing chess and going bowling?"

I suspect that many an older Adventist may also wonder about these things as well! There are many quotes we could list, but here is one that lays out quite clearly her perspective on the way we choose entertainment. She wrote: "I was shown that Sabbathkeepers as a people labor too hard without allowing themselves change or periods of rest. Recreation is needful to those who are engaged in physical labor and is still more essential for those whose labor is principally mental. . . . There are amusements, such as dancing, card playing, chess, checkers, etc., which we cannot approve, because Heaven condemns them. These amusements open the door for great evil. They are not beneficial in their tendency, but have an exciting influence, producing in some minds a passion for those plays which lead to gambling and dissipation. All such plays should be condemned by Christians, and something perfectly harmless should be substituted in their place."[3]

Context matters

To understand precisely what Ellen White was getting at, we need to understand something of the setting and times in which she gave her counsel. Several studies (such as, *The World of Ellen G. White* by Gary Land and *Ellen White's World* by George R. Knight) give some helpful historical context for statements she made about entertainment choices. These scholars point out that most respectable people of Ellen White's time shunned places such as dance halls, pool halls, bowling alleys, and "concert saloons"—many of which were nothing but fronts for prostitution, gambling, drinking, or even criminal gangs. These were places were young people were lured into lives of vice.

The principle Ellen White lays down is clear. She's saying, Stay away from places of entertainment and avoid amusements that will potentially pull you away from your Christian walk and into destructive habits.

It's important to help our young people understand the broad principles that run through Ellen White's counsel, for these are cross-cultural and timeless; they teach us safe and good values. What's the alternative? A numbered list of dos and don'ts may make sense within one time and culture but may be utterly out of place in another. The result? Joyless legalism.

We're custodians of an invaluable treasure—a prophetic ministry that supports us in both our faith and our mission. Do our young people understand how significant this gift is? Do they have a clear, undistorted understanding of Ellen White's function within our faith community? Are their encounters with her writings encouraging and faith building, or merely perplexing? Do they feel free to express their questions or concerns to us?

We owe it to our young people to talk to them about Ellen White and to do everything we possibly can to open up her inspired counsel to their generation.

[Conversation starters]

Do you want to explore more deeply some of the issues raised in this chapter? Here are some ideas for starting a dialogue between younger and older members of your congregation.

1. **Have your say.** What does Ellen White's ministry mean to you? What books, experiences, or people have helped shape your feelings?

2. **Conversation builders.**
   - Adventist scholar George Knight suggests we need to approach Ellen White's writings with common sense, keeping in mind the particular time and culture in which she lived.[4] Can you think of examples of when we've failed to use common sense in interpreting Ellen White's counsels?

   - Imagine a friend or colleague asks you, "Who was Ellen White and what role does she have in your church?" How would you respond?

3. **Discussion questions.**
   - Ellen White herself warned that her counsels shouldn't be treated as an addition to Scripture, but do we sometimes act as if they are?

   - What's the best way to introduce teens to the writings of Ellen White?

   - How do you react to the idea of modern adaptations of Ellen White books, such as Jerry D. Thomas's *Messiah,* which rewrites *The Desire of Ages* in today's language?

What now? Could your congregation be more deliberate in educating young and old alike about the relevance of Ellen White's counsels today? What approaches would best help your young people develop an appreciation for the spiritual treasures her writings offer? (Two online resources to consider are George Knight's short article "Reading Ellen White in the 21st Century"[5] and the White Estate's "Working With Teachers" archive,[6] which lists downloadable teaching material.)

[Endnotes]

1. Ellen G. White, "Search the Scriptures," *Review and Herald,* July 26, 1892.

2. White, *Selected Messages,* 1:37.

3. White, *Testimonies,* 1:514.

4. George R. Knight, *Reading Ellen White: How to Understand and Apply Her Writings* (Hagerstown, Md.: Review and Herald®, 1997), 95.

5. George R. Knight, "Reading Ellen White in the 21st Century," *Adventist World,* November 2009, accessed March 31, 2013, http://www.adventistworld.org/article/655/resources/english/issue-2009-1011/reading-ellen-white-in-the-21st-century.

6. The Ellen G. White Estate's "Working With Teachers" resources can be accessed at http://teachers.ellenwhite.org/.

Twelve

"I Have an Idea!"

[Making Space for Young People]

This is what they said

- *"I have an idea for raising funds for our church through a series of concerts. I've been working on this for a while, but I don't know who to speak to in my conference to really make this happen. Who should I talk to?"*

- *"I'd like to start a program to give low-income people computer training and help them learn new skills. Do you think that would be a good way to connect with the community? I'm not sure if my pastor would be on board, but there are a couple of guys who also go to my church who think this would really work. How would I get something like that started?"*

- *"I think it would benefit everyone—not just young people—to have a leadership skills program once a year in every local church. Sometimes my church struggles to elect leaders, not for lack of talent, but lack of experience or skills."*

- *"Everyone wonders how we can keep young people from leaving through the back door. Here's my answer: community. First we need to create a community among volunteer youth workers, then we need to create a space for them to communicate with each other around the world, then we need to focus on creating a feeling of community among all Adventist youth. We need to help them understand that they belong to something big and that they can truly make a difference."*

- *"I am twenty-three years old. When I look around, I see that we are not really being scientific in the way we equip local churches to share our truths. For instance, every home has a TV and DVD player. Why aren't we producing more high quality graphical programs—like the cartoons of Dreamworks or Disney? This is what people are watching, and this is what they're used to and what they understand. Why can't we focus on things that people are already used to, and use those ways to share eternal truth?"*

- *"We're the MTV generation. We're postmodern. We need to translate our prophetic message into ways that postmodern youth can understand, especially in first world countries where the church feels like it's about to die. Problem is, it's my generation that will need to do the translating because we're the only ones who know the language. I think the General Conference needs to set up an international youth think tank to seriously look at this."*

- *"If you really want to listen to the voices of young people, I'd like to suggest that you create a special youth contingent to be on the floor at General Conference sessions. We'd be able to present a perspective that is not currently being heard, plus we'd be getting amazing experience in church leadership. If we're going to be the leaders of tomorrow, we need to be more involved than just attending youth programs!"*

- *"We need to make the worship service less predictable. You know how it is— three praise songs, two hymns, prayer, sermon. Why don't we say to churches, 'Give one service a month to your young people'—not to do crazy things, but to plan the service in ways that will appeal to younger people and give us a reason to invite our friends to church."*

- *"People sometimes aren't comfortable with young people preaching sermons from the pulpit. Well, here's my solution: encourage young people to preach sermons at parks or other public places! It actually works and it's impressive how people really get into it."*

- *"Here's my idea: Why don't we create a worldwide online network of young adults with an emphasis on mission work? We can swap ideas, report on things that worked (or didn't), and encourage each other when things are difficult. I think church members of my age have the same kinds of challenges no matter where we live."*

- *"Here's what I think will make a difference. Let's put into practice the 'priesthood of all believers.' Let's integrate it into the curriculum of our schools; let's train teachers to talk about spirituality in every academic discipline and teach students that they have a responsibility to put what they know into practice. In our churches, let's focus on getting rid of the clergy/laity separation as much as possible. I think, more than anything, this gives young people the message that they shouldn't/can't get active in their church and community."*

- *"I am lucky because church leaders have always asked me and my friends to take on responsibility. I think this is the biggest issue—young people need to feel that it is expected that they will be involved and make a big contribution. From what I can see, most Adventist young people experience the opposite—older people expect them not to take on responsible positions. What I'm suggesting is that I think our church needs to train adults to expect more from young people!"*

- *"One of the biggest problems I see is that people my age are too fearful to be up front about letting people know they want to get involved or how they think they can contribute. What happens is that the young people sit back and let the elders and deacons pass us by because we haven't spoken up! So an idea I have is: Older people need to be more active in reaching out to young people and finding out if they want to be involved. Sometimes all we need is a bit of a push to get over that first barrier."*

- *"Singing and playing a musical instrument are the 'acceptable' ways young people can be involved in the worship service—but that means that the majority of young people are just expected to sit in the pew. I would like to start a program for local churches that opens up a whole range of other artistic ways for involvement, such as poetry, drama, and mime. (I think this will need to come from the conference or union, because I have no support for this from my church.)"*

- *"I am so proud to be a Seventh-day Adventist and to be part of God's family. People talk about youth today being rebellious or troublemakers, but I think that young people actually are our church's best-kept secret. When young people are committed to something and show it through their actions, then that's when other people really take notice. It's powerful."*

- *I'm an Adventist young person full of vigor and enthusiasm to move the gospel to the ends of the earth. That's why we're here! If we're given a chance, I think young people can be the leaders of today—not just of the future."*

OK, this is what they said—it's just a small sample of some of the big ideas that crossed my desk, or that I heard from young people during the seven-year life of *Let's Talk*. I received countless suggestions—ranging from the inspired to the outrageous—for mission, spiritual growth, community outreach, church restructuring, and worship. What linked all these ideas together, however, was one overarching plea: Include us! We have ideas and energy, and we want to be involved. Please, don't keep us on the sidelines!

What emerged clearly is that young people care about their church, they're thinking about both mission and leadership, and they have well-developed ideas to communicate, many of which are exceptionally creative. What also came through is that their thinking often reflects the postmodern culture into which they were born. Many of their ideas demonstrate their concern to translate our prophetic message into a language that their secular, unchurched peers can understand. Some are asking to have a part in helping redesign worship services to have a greater cross-generational appeal, and their request is simple: "Give us a chance!"

A question of trust

In looking back at my interactions with young people from many different cultures, the strongest and deepest impression that remains with me is that they feel underused and somewhat marginalized in their church. This isn't necessarily by design—it just happens. We love our youth, but do we really trust them? Or do they sense that we view them with a kind of benign suspicion? We can do better than that!

It's time to reexamine the climate in our local congregations and to assess how we're doing in nurturing that most critical value—cross-generational *trust*. Trust ranks above skills and experience. Skills are sharpened over time and develop with practice; and experience—there is only one way you get that. You can't learn to swim by correspondence course. Only by doing a thing, carrying a responsibility, discharging an assignment, do you develop this much sought-after experience that supposedly qualifies you for important leadership roles.

I've learned, however, that no matter how valuable experience is, spiritual gifts, natural talents, and personality are of greater importance when considering leadership assignments within the church. This is just as true in a local congregation as it is in senior leadership levels of global church administration. However experienced, a person with the wrong combination of gifts is always going to be the inappropriate person to lead out.

There are so many young people who have energy, ideas, and spiritual gifts, and who love people and love their church. As you identify these young men and women, set them free to lead. Declare your trust in them, and that's probably all you need to do to start a sea change in your congregation. They won't be reckless. They may be creative and used by the Holy Spirit in ways we can't imagine—and this may challenge those of us who are set in our ways. But no one, young or old, can function well and give their best without trust.

So, what do we have to lose? The under-thirty-five-year-olds make up more than 50 percent of our church membership, and too many are failing to thrive in the climate of their local church—so they're walking away. The tragedy is that they see no reason to stay. We have to give highest priority to this loss. While freedom will always have its casualties, the bleeding we're experiencing now must be fixed—or at least, we must try.

A tale of two worlds

The cover article of a magazine I picked up the other day featured an extensive interview with young entrepreneur-inventor-businessman Jack Dorsey. He came from nowhere, worked at one point as a massage therapist, and lived in a shed of about sixty square feet in a friend's backyard. By the age of thirty-five, he was a multibillionaire and creator of the social networking phenomenon Twitter and CEO of mobile payments company Square. What other goals does he have? He'd like to follow Michael Bloomberg as mayor of New York City.

This is the world our young people and young professionals understand. It's a world where the ability of young people to navigate the new technological landscape is recognized, celebrated, and eagerly sought. Young entrepreneurs such as Dorsey and Facebook's Mark Zuckerberg have ushered in an era of high-profile, youth-led dominance in technology, media, communication, and business. Even the world of politics seems today to be largely powered by the energy, ideas, and skills of young people. Crucial to United States President Barack Obama's 2012 election campaign, for instance, were his cadre of dedicated young number-crunchers, bloggers, and social-media strategists.

What does this mean for our church today? For a start, it means that there's often a striking disparity between young people's reality at work and in their everyday lives, and what they encounter when they walk through the church doors each Sabbath.

In the secular world, the phenomenon of youth achievement and competence is a given. But what dominant narrative do young people find within their church? Too often, they encounter an implied message that they're incapable or troublemakers or irrelevant when it comes to leadership within their local church community. In short, that their elders would prefer they be seen but not heard.

An alternate energy source?

Young people are there, waiting in the pews (at least, for now). Are we stubbornly refusing to recognize one of the most powerful resources for mission God has given to His church?

Our young people know they need to help the church look at some things differently and perhaps try some new approaches in order to reach the very secular, postmodern world they inhabit. They represent our best hope for making our mission more effective within a cultural milieu that, for some of us, could just as well belong to a different universe.

Young people can also bring a freshness of perspective to our church's organizational culture. I was interested to read in the *Forbes* magazine profile of Jack Dorsey that he credits the success of his two companies, Twitter and Square, to two key values: transparency and trust. "Dorsey is insistent that everyone who works for him knows what the company is up to and why it is doing it," the article reveals. "So he instituted an astonishing rule at Square: At every meeting involving more than two people, someone must take notes—and send them to the entire staff."[1]

That's not a bad idea for a church that has a strong interest in developing an ethos of openness and transparency!

For Dorsey and for young people generally, openness allows ideas to travel and meet; ideas and people talk to each other—and serendipity happens. Age isn't a hindrance as long as the right mind-set is there and ideas are given a chance to either thrive or die. This is how it happens today in so many areas of art, culture, and business, and it can happen also in the church if we're willing to try.

In terms of age and experience, our young professionals of today are probably where the disciples of our Lord were when He selected them. Our young people are where most of our early pioneers were during the early days of the Advent awakening. These early Adventists made mistakes both in leadership and in their understanding of mission and Scripture, but the Spirit was with them and brought them safely through difficult periods. Making mistakes doesn't disqualify good people. Instead, good people learn from their mistakes and you move on to better things.

Time to take action

So, this is where we are: 50 percent (or more) of our church family is youth and young professionals, and many have a family with small children. They represent an almost endless supply of ideas, talents, and energy. And, in addition to what their secular counterparts have, they're also endowed with spiritual gifts. They're experiencing the outpouring of the Holy Spirit, and they dream dreams and see visions (Joel 2:28, 29).

What can we do to make sure these assets flow into the life and witness of the church? It will only happen by *deliberate planning*—we've tried everything else, and it hasn't worked.

So how could a local church implement a deliberate plan for youth engagement?

To be deliberate, a plan must be formalized—that is, actions and decisions must be taken, voted on, and in some instances documented in written form as an authorization for action. There must be broad-based consultation with all constituencies within a church—a model imposed from an outside higher organization will never work. The initiative must be local-constituency owned.

Let's consider two possible models. They both aim to engage youth and young professionals in the church, but take different approaches.

- A deliberate effort to include young people as members of planning committees, executive committees, and boards of church-owned organizations or entities; and,

- a deliberate effort to empower young people to carry elected leadership of local congregations.

1. Small steps forward

Let's take a closer look at the first proposal. It's not as if we haven't already made efforts to bring more young men and women to membership of committees with executive functions; it's just that these efforts haven't really moved us beyond tokenism.

Admittedly, there are significant structural limitations. For instance, a member of an institutional board or executive committee is often there by virtue of the position he or she holds in church-employed leadership. And committee membership is generally outlined in various by-laws or working policies that are legally fixed—unless those entities take the initiative to change these provisions. Church constituencies, then, are limited in their ability to select lay representatives for different committees.

Yes, we could insert a clause that says some of the lay representatives on a board or executive committee must be young professionals who aren't employed by the church. This would, in the interest of openness, need to be spelled out in the by-laws of the organization. The number may be small, but it would be a step forward. Even though we already have some church-employed young professionals on many key committees (for example, conference officers), they don't bring quite the same experience and perspective as would young professionals who work in a secular environment.

Since 2005, the General Conference has made concerted efforts to bring young professionals—laypeople—into its Executive Committee, and there are now approximately thirty young members, nine of whom are women.

But we need to do more. I believe we need an up-front, defined formula for selecting young people for representative functions within the church. If a plan isn't in place, it becomes a decision of the moment, subject to all manner of different influences or personal considerations. And that is *not* a trust-creating basis on which to proceed.

If all this seems a somewhat slow and cumbersome process for empowering young people in our church, it's because it *is* slow and cumbersome. It's a vital, but necessarily drawn-out process. Is there something more we could do?

2. A radical proposal

What would happen if a local congregation made up of young and old, married and singles, were to make a radical change in the elected leadership positions of their congregation? What if they were to decide that for a two-year period, or some other defined time—the elected leadership positions of their church, such as elders and deacons, were only to be filled by individuals under-thirty-five years of age?

I can almost hear gasps of horror. "What church would possibly want to accept the imposition of such an idea?" some may ask. The answer is probably not a single one! This could never work as an imposition from outside. It could work only if a local church decided for itself—a decision of the senior church members as much as of the younger. Together, they would have to agree to spread the range of responsibilities differently in their church, at least for a while.

Those who've faithfully and cheerfully carried leadership responsibilities in their church for years would temporarily take on new roles—that of mentors and supporters of a younger generation of local church leaders. And the pastoral staff would simply continue to function in the same way as they did before.

Wouldn't such a decisive and deliberate move be worth the risk to see if there's any value in it? Wouldn't it be worth finding out? We'd discover how this change might transform the internal workings of a congregation, particularly in terms of the engagement of the younger families. We could also see new outreach ideas take hold, potentially transforming the church's relationship to its community and the way it undertakes mission. I believe we'd also see a change in the flavor of a congregation's worship experience in ways that would enrich—not distort—the biblical message and Adventist identity.

But let me be absolutely clear: this would never work unless a local congregation itself—young and old together—enthusiastically embraced the idea.

What are the risks? I see no risks that aren't far outweighed by benefits. I suspect we'd discover how responsibly and thoughtfully the younger generation would look after their church and sharpen the church's tools for mission. We'd be releasing a generation of Adventist youth into the public life of the church where they may have previously been all but silent. I believe we'd discover that young adults are, by and large, extremely loyal and protective of their church. It's their church, and their own future is tied to it.

I can still hear the words of a young man, just twenty-one years of age, after he'd preached the Sabbath morning sermon in a city where the church has a huge challenge. He said to me, "I will never allow my church in this secular city to go down on my watch!"

I believe unreserved trust and mutual support between young and old in our churches may, through the reconciling ministry of Holy Spirit, take us to a new day and experience that we've longed for, but haven't yet been able to bring about. Shouldn't we try it?

[Conversation starters]

Do you want to explore more deeply some of the issues raised in this chapter? Here are some ideas for starting a dialogue between younger and older members of your congregation.

1. **Have your say.** What do you think would happen in your congregation if, for a certain length of time, all elected leadership positions were filled by those under the age of thirty-five?

2. **Conversation builders.**
   - According to Christian blogger Adam Copeland, "Making a congregation welcoming for young adults necessarily means it will become less comfortable for the current members."[2] Do you agree?

   - According to one young Adventist, "[Young people] get lazy, we go to the big churches where our friends are at and come to the service and go back home and just chill on the Sabbath."[3] Are young people allowing themselves to be sidelined? How could young people be more assertive about seeking leadership roles?

3. **Discussion questions.**
   - Is your church a place where young people are likely to feel at home? On a scale of 1 to 10, how would you rate how your church's efforts to create a welcoming environment for under-thirty-fives?

   - What are some key characteristics of a youth-friendly church?

   - Are there certain attitudes or traditions within your congregation that make it difficult for leaders to hand over meaningful responsibility to younger members?

   - What unique strengths do you think young people would bring to leadership roles? Any liabilities?

What now? Is your church ready to be more intentional about giving young people more leadership responsibility?
   - What are some practical steps you could take to empower your under-thirty-fives?

   - What goals would be realistic for your congregation?

[Endnotes]

1. Eric Savitz, "Jack Dorsey: Leadership Secrets of Twitter and Square," *Forbes,* November 5, 2012, accessed December 4, 2012, http://www.forbes.com/sites/ericsavitz/2012/10/17/jack -dorsey-the-leadership-secrets-of-twitter-and-square/3/.

2. Adam J. Copeland, "Reaching Out to Young Adults Will Screw Up Your Church," *A Wee Blether* (blog), May 24, 2012, accessed November 22, 2012, http://www.adamjcopeland.com /2012/05/24/reaching-out-to-young-adults-will-screw-up-your-church.

3. Tumblr entry by Mumu14, "Mainstream Christianity," accessed November 28, 2012, http:// www.tumblr.com/tagged/seventh-day-adventist?before=1294635251.

What I Learned From the Young

For many years, I lived within academic communities—in Africa, Germany, the United States, and England. It's difficult to imagine a more dynamic, creative, or energetic environment than an institution of higher learning where young, inquisitive minds are absorbing, processing, and retesting ideas—both inside and outside the classrooms. I sometimes found that the classical definition of *teacher* and *student* were reversed, and I experienced the academic equivalent of what any parent will recognize as the things-we-inherit-from-our-kids syndrome.

For me, the experience of *Let's Talk* continued that process. These conversations were international and multicultural and reflected so many different flavors of Adventist youth culture. Through our conversations, these young men and women not only shared their thoughts and feelings but also challenged me to keep an eye on some of my *own* attitudes.

1. Young people taught me the value of openness.

The beauty of the young mind is that it comes to the process of discovery without a bunch of hang-ups and locked-in positions. I'm not suggesting that our young people aren't, on the whole, clear about what they believe, or that they don't hold to core principles. But young people also possess an urge—a hunger— to find things out for themselves. They have a yearning for freshness, a desire to look openly at everything they encounter and to develop a sense of personal ownership of their faith.

For this, you need an open mind that looks critically at ideas and information and considers different perspectives. You have to approach intellectual inquiry without fear. (Fear comes later, after you've burnt your fingers in the process of discovery or in communicating to others what you've found.)

How will young people react if their partners in conversation come to them with closed minds, seeking to coerce rather than engage? They'll step back, and meaningful communication will become impossible.

2. Young people taught me that human beings are more important than knowledge.

Being kind is more important than winning a debate about rights and wrongs. We may be able to eloquently defend many positions, statements, and opinions. We may be skilled in interpreting God's Word. But it's all meaningless unless we're actually helping guide men and women into God's future.

At the end of the day, the only thing that really matters is the salvation of individual sinners, each one deeply loved by God. Remember, it's *people,* not ideas, who will inhabit the earth made new. Perhaps we need to sit back for a while and let this thought really sink in. It's an obvious fact that we too often contradict our statements by our actions and attitudes.

Young people also taught me, as a theologian, to remember that theology has no independent right to exist. Its value lies solely in its ability to lead people to Christ and bring them into the secure embrace of an everlasting and almighty God. And then, it's from the safety of His arms that we can let our minds probe deeper into divine mysteries.

3. Young people taught me it's critical to keep the conversation going.

According to some marriage therapists, the most dangerous period for a relationship isn't when couples are arguing, it's when indifference takes over and communication ceases. So it is with our spiritual family.

It can be extraordinarily difficult to keep communication alive with those who are divided from us by age, experiences, or expectations. We find it far more comfortable to chat with like-minded people whose chemistry and assumptions line up with ours. But at the end of the conversation, what did we accomplish? Did we learn or grow? No, we haven't explored new ideas; we've simply encouraged our preexisting ideas to congeal. A strong, active, and open mind will never be satisfied with that.

So, how do we keep the conversation alive? Young people have taught me that there are a number of guaranteed conversation killers we should avoid at all costs.

Communication will come to a grinding halt, for instance, if we fail to extend to each other the courtesy of trust. Any discussion is doomed from the outset if either party thinks, or implies, that the other is being disingenuous, unnecessarily provocative, or deliberately thickheaded. We have to be willing to accept each other's sincerity. This is fundamental, yet it's often so difficult! It doesn't mean giving up our own opinions—but it does mean acknowledging the right of other people to hold a different point of view.

Perhaps we also limit communication between generations in our church by assuming that conversation is pointless unless it brings us to a resolution. Agreement may or may not come, and that's OK. Living with tensions and differences is simply a reality of membership in the body of Christ. Through the years the young have taught me the tremendous rewards of keeping the conversation going, even when there's no clear destination in sight. They didn't expect me to always have the answers. What they valued far more was genuine interest, a commitment of time and effort, and a willingness to engage with the issues they brought to the table.

4. Young people taught me to restrain my "superior knowledge."

As a young college professor, some of my students brought out the best in me; some of them brought out the worst. One student who definitely fell into the latter category once said to me: "Perhaps my little knowledge has made me ignorant, but your greater knowledge has made you arrogant."

I found one class particularly challenging. There were four or five students in the class and each one had a good, inquiring mind. Yet, from the paranoid perspective of a teacher, it sometimes felt like they'd schemed together to make my life difficult.

One day I walked out of the class and said to a colleague in the hallway, "I'm absolutely fed up with this class—especially with the ones who seem to have stayed up the night before every class thinking up the most negative, critical questions they can throw at me. From now on, I'm just going to give them the theology straight, toss in a few Greek and Latin formulae for good measure. They can sort themselves out and face the hour of judgment on examination day."

My colleague said, "That's probably not a good idea. Just give them time and let them talk. You don't have to have an answer to every question, but talking is better than silence."

He was right. My students didn't need to be just given the right answers; what they really needed was the space and time to work toward these answers for themselves.

Those of us from the older generations must never wield our "superior" knowledge like a trump card that can be thrown down whenever we want to cut off discussion. The silence that follows won't be the silence of agreement; it'll be the sound of minds closing, attitudes hardening, and communication coming to an abrupt end.

5. Young people taught me not to be too severe.

I'll never forget one particular young woman I encountered during my time as president of Newbold College in England. She was a handful, and then some.

She'd driven her residence hall dean to the brink and had tested me in the process. In the minds of many people, some of her off-campus activities probably justified expulsion. She had compromised herself.

I met her again decades later. Now a fine professional, committed to the Lord, and supportive of her church, she could look back on her youthful indiscretions and be thankful the chapter didn't end there. As we talked, she reminded me of an incident I'd long forgotten.

"I know I was rebellious and difficult, and I probably tested you to the limit and beyond," she said. "One day, I was standing in the foyer of the main administration building laughing with a couple of my friends. I saw you come in the door at the far end of the building, and I knew there was nowhere for me to escape. Why should I need to escape? Because I was a sight to behold! I had colored my hair bright green. I thought, *Now I've had it!* I'd already overspent my quota of goodwill, and I was sure I'd be shipped out in the morning.

"You walked up to me, stopped, looked at me and said, 'Well, I suppose also that is possible,' and then you just walked away."

She reminded me of this and thanked me for allowing a rebellious kid to live and find herself.

Sometimes kids are kids, and they do stupid things, and often they learn more from their mistakes and stumbles than from anything we can tell them.

6. Young people taught me to exercise the gift of remembering.

At Newbold College in the 1970s, there was still a functioning farm connected with the college. One morning as I entered the worship hall, I was confronted by a cow tied to the pulpit. On another morning, a Morris Minor was parked on the platform. I suspect that neither beast nor car had been brought into the hall as an "offering unto the Lord."

On another occasion a student found his way into the board room and placed stink bombs under the legs of some of the chairs, making the subsequent meeting of the college board an interesting and memorable occasion.

The young have often reminded me that life is made up of all kinds of moments, and not all of them should be serious. Yes, sometimes kids are irresponsible or worse. But we all need to exercise our memories; each one of us was young once, and yet somehow, miraculously, we've grown and moved on. So will today's young Adventist men and women.

7. Young people taught me that my "access" to the mind of God isn't necessarily better than theirs.

Through the years, I've held many elected offices and I can attest to the fact that status within the church doesn't suddenly endow you with the ability to know the mind of God.

Do we who are older and "wiser" sometimes act as if we've earned an inside track to the Divine? That we now have the right to interpret His will for others?

When I taught theology students, conference presidents would regularly stop by my classroom to meet and inspect their future ministerial candidates, and often they'd ask my opinion of the various students.

I had one student I believed wasn't at all suited for the ministry. I'd arrived at that conclusion mainly because I didn't think he had the intellectual ability to grasp some important concepts, and I felt his classroom performance amply backed up my opinion.

I'd spoken to this student about my concerns, and he was sure I was wrong. He was adamant that God had called him to the ministry and I shouldn't question either the existence or the strength of this call.

Several years later, I left Newbold College and I lost track of him, until one day he sent me an invitation to come and preach at his church.

When I arrived, I found that my former student was running an energetic and successful ministry. Over lunch, he graciously reminded me that some fifteen years earlier I'd questioned his calling to ministry. He hadn't forgotten. There wasn't anything triumphalist in his comments, but he did have a smile on his face.

It was clear to me that God was blessing his work, and I had to admit this young man had probably been right about the strength of his calling. Perhaps it was a good reminder to me that God can do amazing things with modest material. But the more important lesson I learned was that I didn't have a more ready, reliable access to God's mind than did the struggling student who'd sat in my classroom.

God is free to speak and guide as He wishes, and He does so constantly in the lives of His servants. But all us, young and old, need to remember that our clearest and safest guidance from Him comes through His Written Word—the Bible. That is how God speaks to our understanding and talks to the community of faith. Any notion of a private revelation—"God spoke to me at four o'clock this morning"—can be highly subjective and ultimately dangerous.

Yes, it's always possible that the Almighty One can communicate in many different ways with His children. But if you claim a private revelation from God, you leave yourself vulnerable to a whole spectrum of dangers.

Our touchstone must always be God's objective Word—a reference point that can be seen by all and which will always give us the clearest, safest revelation of God's purpose for His community and for each of us, personally.

One lesson above all

As I look back, I'm struck by the richness, beauty, and balance of what young

LET'S TALK

Adventist men and women have taught me through the years. Through our conversations, I continually met my Master Teacher, who never tired of teaching and reteaching me the immense value of every person for whom He died. For that, I love Him more than I can describe, and I love the young people of this church who've helped me understand that this is the most important lesson of all.

Where Are We Going?

Jan Paulsen

We have nothing to fear for the future, except as we shall forget the way the Lord has led us, and His teaching in our past history.
—Ellen G. White, Life Sketches, 196

Do we know where we are going and why? Are we focused on the task at hand, or have distractions drawn us away from the priorities to which Christ has called us?

This book isn't advice recycled from other books. Instead, Elder Paulsen shares here the perspectives on leadership he's developed through a lifetime of service. He gives us a series of reflections on issues that are important to our church today and tomorrow. Issues such as the role of women in ministry; the loss of our young people, particularly young professionals; the "us" and "them" of Adventists and other Christan believers; how God views other religions, and what that means for us; how we can preserve unity; and much more.

Leaders experience more than their share of pain and vulnerability. But we can have a tremendous sense of purpose, joy, and fulfillment, because no matter what circumstances we face, we can be sure of the abiding presence of our Lord!

Paperback, 128 Pages
ISBN 13: 978-0-8163-2509-2
ISBN 10: 0-8163-2509-X

Pacific Press®
Publishing Association
"Where the Word Is Life"

Three ways to order:

1	Local	Adventist Book Center®
2	Call	1-800-765-6955
3	Shop	AdventistBookCenter.com